Presenting Yourself

Eastman Kodak Company

Coordinating Editor: Jacalyn R. Salitan
Marketing Director: Jeffrey J. Pollock
Production Coordinator: Elisabeth J. Riedman

John Wiley & Sons Inc, Publishers

Executive Editor: Alan B. Lesure
Marketing Manager: Joseph F. Morse
Production Coordinator: Dennis Gibbons

Library of Congress Catalog Card No. 82-13668

ISBN 0-471-87559-7

Library of Congress Cataloging in Publication Data

Kenny, Michael F.
Presenting yourself.
Includes index.
1. Public speaking. 2. Communication in management.
I. Eastman Kodak Company. II. Title.
PN4121.K344 1982 808.5'1 82-13668
ISBN 0-471-87559-7

Cover and book design: Bill Buckett Associates Inc.
Cover photography: Steven Labuzetta

Printed in the United States of America

10 9 8 7 6 5 4 3 2 1

Presenting Yourself

by Michael Kenny for Eastman Kodak Company

John Wiley & Sons, Inc., Publishers, New York, New York

Contents

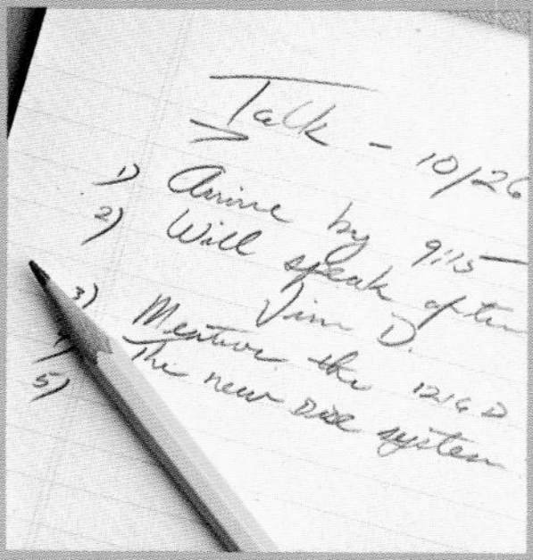

Introduction: The Art of Preparation

If you've ever made a presentation to an audience, you know what this book is about.

It's about the butterflies in your stomach, the dryness of your mouth, and the tightness in your throat as you wait to speak.

It's about all those people looking at you—you would probably say *staring* at you—with their eyes seemingly filled with questions about your ideas as well as your ability.

It's about the audience's probable reaction to your presentation. Will they accept your ideas, buy your product, vote for your candidate or proposal, take up your cause?

In short, this book is about all the anxieties a speaker faces before he or she faces an audience. Yes, anxieties, because if you're like most people, you don't relish the idea of addressing an audience. "Making presentations is not a natural activity for anyone," writes Frank Snell in his book, *How to Stand Up and Speak Well in Business*. He should know. As vice-president of Batten, Barton, Durstine & Osborn, Inc., one of the world's largest advertising agencies, Snell had to overcome this natural discomfort so he could make presentations on a regular basis. According to Snell, the cause of anxiety in most presenters is a feeling of being separated from the audience. The person feels singled out, fears rejection, and desires acceptance and approval. In Snell's words, the inexperienced presenter comes before an audience in a situation perceived as "me versus them."

But it doesn't have to be that way. While it's impossible to eliminate all the anxieties that accompany making a presentation (there's always some nervous excitement present), it is possible to rid yourself of most of them and minimize the paralyzing influence of the rest. The way to do this, writes Snell, is simple: "You must prepare."

So, in a more positive sense, that's what this book is about: the art of preparation. It's about the steps you can take to present yourself, your ideas, and your visuals as effectively as possible. It's about the ways you can get yourself ready—mentally, physically, emotionally and, when you use visuals, technically—to present your ideas so you achieve results. Once you're ready—once you know you have yourself, your material, and the setting under control—your anxieties will dissolve into little more than nervous anticipation, the excitement every athlete or performer feels before the start of an event.

But you have to know how to start—how to prepare to prepare. You have to know what steps to take—and in what order to take them—to make your preparations as efficient and effective as possible. To help you plot and follow these steps, this book will examine the key elements that go into a successful presentation: The presenter; the message, media and methods; and the equipment.

Preparations Begin With You

We'll start with you. You can write a spell-binding script (or have one written). You can produce dramatic visuals (or have them produced). You can plan your logistics and arrangements with the skill of an award-winning director. But if you haven't prepared yourself—if you haven't set goals that mean something to you personally—your presentation stands only a slim chance of success.

You have to prepare yourself. You have to see yourself as "someone worth listening to." You can't approach the presentation with hesitation and doubt. You have to believe in yourself and your abilities, because if you don't no audience will either.

This isn't a suggestion that you become vainglorious. Instead, to quote Frank Snell again, it's a suggestion that you "imagine that you're a leader and in control." Another expert in making presentations is Alfred Tack, director of the Tack School of Public Speaking. In his book, *How To Speak Well in Public,* Tack writes you must see yourself as someone who likes to help others. "If you can't help, inspire, entertain, inform, or persuade others," he writes, "don't give a talk."

And don't expect much in the way of career advancement, either. Tack didn't write that, but he could have, because the ability to communicate to audiences is becoming increasingly a measure of organizational effectiveness. *Fortune* magazine reports that business is searching for what it labels "interpersonal communications consultants," people who teach clients how to give talks and how to project in a forceful, convincing manner. The reasons people go to these consultants, reports *Fortune*, are to sound more confident and persuasive, to dress more effectively, and to attract favorable attention by engaging in outside activities such as giving presentations.

This book can't take the place of these consultants, but it can help you become more effective in projecting your ideas and yourself "in a forceful, convincing manner."

Message, Media, and Methods

You'll also examine the preparations needed to develop the components of your presentation. You'll study more closely the role of objectives and planning in the communication process. You'll learn why it's just as important to know what your audience wants to hear as it is to know what you want to say. You'll examine the single most important criterion for judging the success of a presentation. And once you learn how to set a target for your presentation, you'll learn how to hit it—how to prepare the ideas, words, and other visual materials you'll need to get results.

To make an effective presentation, you must start with effective preparations.

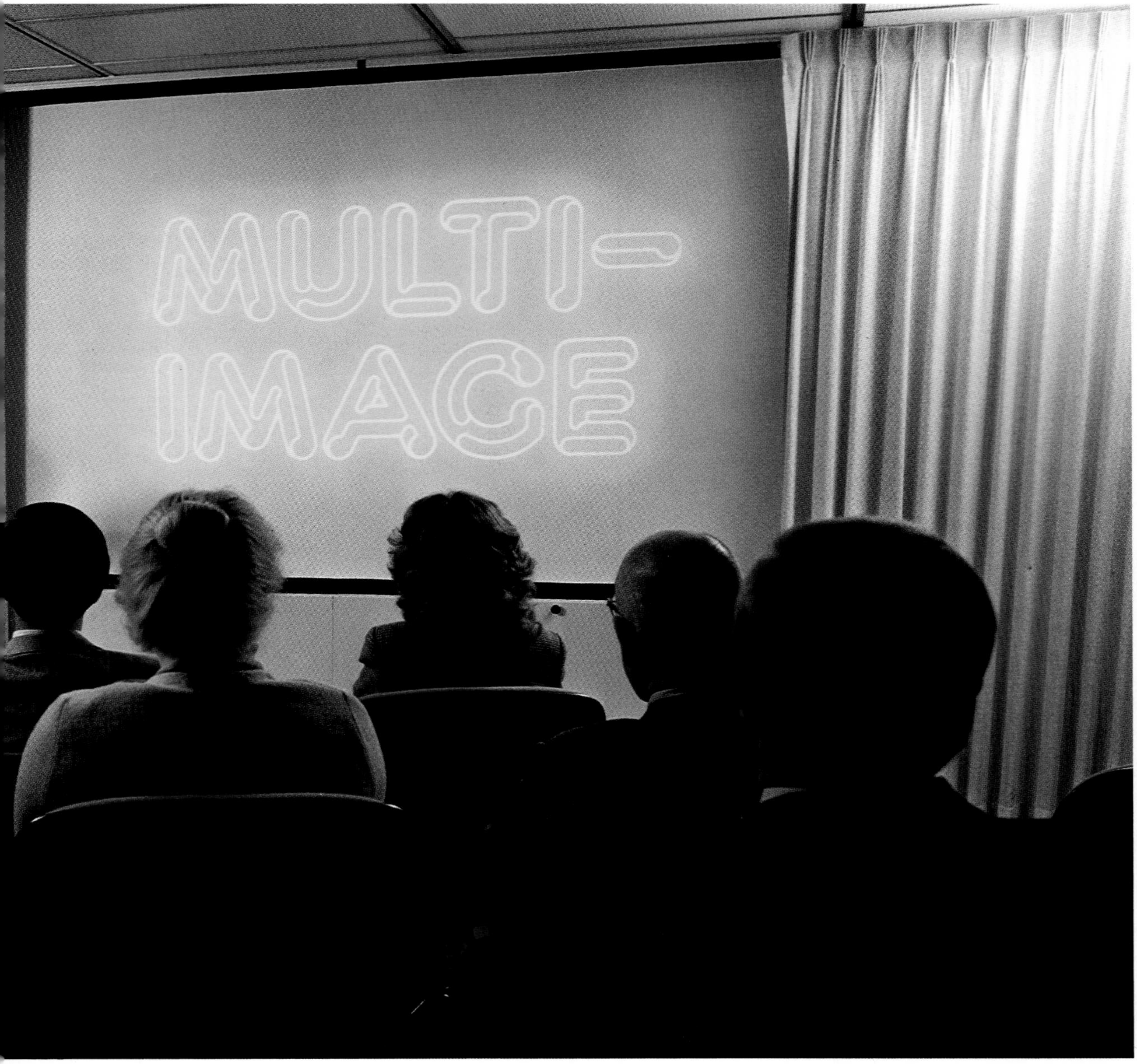
MULTI-
IMAGE

In addition to examining overriding concerns, you'll look at some of the nuts-and-bolts issues that must be considered when preparing a presentation. Should you use a prepared text, notes, or just trust your memory? What should you look for in the arrangements and setting for your presentation (or how should you plan for them if you're in control)? Should you rehearse your presentation? How often? And with whom?

But perhaps the most important part of this examination of message, media, and methods will deal with the use of visuals in a presentation. This emphasis on visual communication stems from the somewhat paradoxical nature of human communication. Most of our communication with each other is verbal. We bombard each other with words, some of them written, but the overwhelming majority of them are spoken. We talk, talk, talk–while eating, while driving, while problem-solving, while entertaining; across a table, across a room, across a convention hall; in person, over radio, with tapes, over television. We're flooded with words, with talk. It's our natural way of communicating.

But it's not our most effective or efficient way. Experts on communication have estimated that we understand–comprehend–only about 25 percent of what we hear. On the other hand, most of what we learn comes to us through sight, through visual communication of one form or another. It starts when we're infants; for the first year of life we're constantly watching and imitating–learning visually. We see, we do, we fail, we correct, and try again. When we go to school, the process continues. Our teachers instruct us with spoken words, but much of what we learn we see in books, in pictures, on maps, and in slide and movie presentations.

So given our extensive verbal background, it's not unusual that when asked to give a presentation we think first about the words we're going to speak. "What will I say?" becomes the primary question, overlooking the fact that most of what our audience will understand and remember is rooted in visual media. In fact, some psychologists claim that even when you try to recall some-

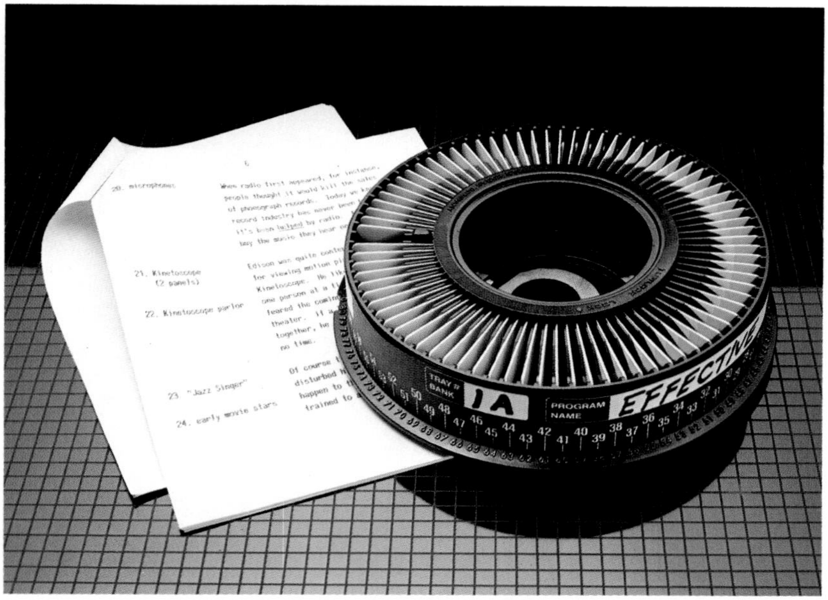

If you want an audience to comprehend and remember your message, present it using both words *and* visuals.

COMMUNICATIONS
SATELLITES

one's words, you will more than likely begin by forming a visual image in your mind of the occasion when the words were spoken. Then you will look and listen as you try to recall the conversation. So if our audiences remember more of what they see than of what they hear, we should devote as much, if not more, attention to what we can show them.

But while speaking is a natural act, planning, preparing, and presenting visuals are not. It takes some training before you know what works and what doesn't. So this book will examine in detail the steps you should take to prepare the visuals for your presentations.

Equipment

How will you present your message? With slides, film, displays? Using photography, graphics, or art? Using a single tabletop projector or a computer-controlled array of projectors?

To answer these questions, you'll have to examine the role of equipment in a presentation. You'll also have to look at the physical and human resources you'll need at the presentation site to help synchronize your verbal and visual messages. And you'll have to study the factors to be considered when making a presentation at a number of sites.

The Approach

Our approach in analyzing these elements of a presentation will be to examine them in a chronological sequence, starting with analyzing an audience and setting objectives, then moving through the various production sequences until we arrive at rehearsal and the actual presentation. Remember, however, that there's no one "accepted" sequence of production to be followed without deviation. The sequence we suggest is a common one, but it allows for many variations. Our advice is this: if you haven't developed a production sequence that you're comfortable with, try ours the first few times you prepare and give a presentation. But experiment with it, modify it, change it in any way that will make it *your* production sequence. This isn't a recipe book, it's a guide. Use it in any way that serves you best.

The Presentation Room

The final section of this book examines a special aspect of preparing for presentations. If you or your organization deliver numerous presentations over the course of a year, you might consider building a presentation room.

A presentation room is just what the name suggests: a room set aside and equipped for presentations. For all intents and purposes, it's a miniature theatre: sufficient and comfortable seating; a lectern or some other suitable structure at which a speaker can stand; a projection room equipped with slide and film projectors, tape recorders, and other audiovisual equipment; suitable acoustics; and screens on which to project images.

This book will help you decide if you need such a room. And if the answer is yes, you'll find useful recommendations to help you design and construct your room, working with a budget determined by your presentation requirements.

Other Help

Now that you know what this book *will* cover, let's look briefly at what it doesn't.

This book isn't a course on public speaking or speechmaking. If your objective is to give talks, to stand before an audience and entertain them or inform them or lead them with the power of words alone, you'll need to turn elsewhere for assistance and coaching.

As mentioned before, there are a growing number of organizations that will, for a fee, help you improve your public speaking skills. According to a report in *Business Week* magazine, among the more sophisticated and ambitious of these organizations are Arthur W. Sager Associates, Inc., of Topsfield, Massachusetts; the Executive Technique, of Chicago, and Communispond, Inc., of New York City.

If your goals are more modest, you might try the Dale Carnegie Institute. Or you can write to Toastmasters International (P.O. Box 10400, Santa Ana, California 92711) for the address of the local branch of this grassroots public speaking organization.

In the appendix of this book you'll also find a bibliography of books on public speaking. If you have little experience in giving talks or presentations, you might want to read one or more of these books. All are good guides to the do's and don'ts of public speaking; as such, they can give you the background you need to fully appreciate and use the techniques presented in this book.

1 Setting Objectives, Getting Results

Ed, a salesman with a business equipment firm, makes a presentation to the financial managers of a young corporation whose sales last year just topped $500,000. He tells them how his company's machines helped save Corporation X more than a quarter of a million dollars last year. How Company Y consolidated several financial functions into one operation. How Company Z speeds financial reports to managers throughout the world. His presentation is concise, factual, emphatic. Yet when it's over, the financial managers thank him politely and send him on his way.

Martha, an executive with a major retailing organization, makes a presentation to women business leaders at a convention focusing on "Women in Business: The Next Plateau." Her presentation concentrates on the problems she faced in overcoming the stereotype of "female salesclerk." Her presentation is factual, charged with emotion, and backed with visuals. But when she's through, the audience applauds politely and wanders off to other convention activities.

Robert, an audiovisual specialist with a major government agency, gives a multi-image presentation stressing the importance of investment in public transportation to a group of local government and business leaders. His 40-minute presentation is filled with dramatic slides and film clips, lively music and sound effects, and is programmed to produce dazzling screen effects. But, when the lights go up, he answers a few polite questions and the audience quickly leaves, grumbling among themselves about wasting time during a busy day.

Recognize these people? Chances are you do. Maybe you've sat through similar presentations made by their real-life counterparts, wondering what you had to gain from your investment of time.

Or maybe you recognize Ed, Martha, or Robert because you've been in their shoes. After hours of work, fretting, and anxiety, you stand before an audience–and miss your mark. You hear the applause, but you know your listeners are only being polite. Or you get a thank-you and a firm handshake–but no order. Again you wonder if the investment of time has been worth it.

Of course, no matter what situation you've found yourself in, you're not alone. Unfortunately, we've all wasted time with presentations–as a speaker, an audience member, or both. And the reason we've wasted time is because most people don't know how to prepare for a presentation. If all speakers knew how to get under way–if they knew that producing and giving a presentation was like building a house, an act requiring a definite progression of sequential steps–there would be far fewer bored audiences and far more successful presenters.

That knowledge, however, does not come with the gift of speech, although a great many people seem to think it does. They think that just because they're "good on their feet," because they "like" to talk to people, that they can automatically make an effective presentation.

Maybe they can; maybe they can't. It's helpful to be articulate and at ease in front of people, but those qualities don't necessarily guarantee success when it comes to making presentations. Presentations are a special sort of communications, a hybrid somewhere between a political speech and a television commercial. The goal is always to influence people, through the power of your ideas, your tone of voice, the force of your gestures, as well as through the impact of visuals. And the performance—the presentation itself—is as far removed from ordinary conversation as humming in the shower is from singing at the Met.

So being articulate and comfortable are advantages, but they're not requisite attributes. The one quality that is required for a successful presenter is the propagandist's insistence on results. When you give a presentation, you have to create a change in your audience. In fact, this is the single, most important criterion for an effective presentation: *The audience must respond in a way (or ways) determined by you.*

That means applause and polite thank-yous don't count—unless, of course, all you want for your effort is applause and a thank-you. More than likely, however, you want more than that. You want audiences to feel a certain emotion, or think a specific thought, or perform a particular act. It's achieving these results that makes the work that goes into producing and giving a presentation worthwhile.

To be a successful presenter, you must first set well defined communications objectives.

Preparation: The Key to Success

So the key to making a successful presentation is to learn to set a target and hit it. Read that sentence again, because that's what this entire book is about. *Set a target. And hit it.* If you take away nothing else from this book but the determination to follow those two directives, you'll make much better presentations than you do now.

Set a target.

And hit it.

Of course, this breakdown is obvious; everyone knows you first set a target, then hit it. But knowledge isn't practice, and the most common practice for inexperienced presenters is to plunge right into the second phase of preparation.

They want to hit their target. So they select a topic or theme; research the subject; write and rewrite the script; and if the presentation is to have visuals, they have slides shot and loaded into slide trays. They may even have their visual sequences programmed. And then they rehearse, go off to their presentation—and miss the target.

And wonder why.

The answer is paradoxical: They miss their target because they try too hard to hit it *in the first place.* They overlook the entire process that goes into setting a target, the operation that correctly belongs *in the first place.*

Setting a target is the first–and the most critical–phase of preparation. The analysis and planning that go into setting a target tell you what you want to accomplish and suggest the most effective means of achieving your goal. When you know how you want your audience to respond, you can then decide what themes and what media you can use to trigger that response.

Setting a target means developing a set of objectives. These objectives are of two sorts. The first and most important we've already mentioned: statements of the response you want to produce in an audience. We'll refer to them as communications objectives. The second type of objective deals with production values: Decisions relating to the use of visuals, the types of visuals to be used, the length of your presentation, the most desirable setting for the presentation, and so on. To keep these production objectives distinct from the more important

Some Final Questions

"You're probably wondering what brings me before you today."

So goes the speaker's old gag line. Only we suggest you take it seriously. Before you accept an invitation to give a presentation (or look for a forum for a presentation you have in mind), ask yourself, "Why am I doing this? Is it really worth the time and effort I'll have to invest?"

One way to answer those questions is to review your work sheet on Setting Your Objectives. When you do, try to decide, as best you can, if indeed you can achieve your objectives given the nature and motivations of your audience.

If your objective is to convince your audience to buy a 550-horsepower six-miles-to-the-gallon sports car, and your audience consists of conservationists motivated by a desire to cut the consumption of gasoline by Americans, you're undoubtedly wasting your time. No matter how effective you are as a presenter, no matter how dramatic and dazzling your visuals, you're not likely to swing an audience 180 degrees in its thinking. So save your time and energy.

Of course, no set of communications objectives or analysis of an audience can give you an infallible answer to the question of whether or not you'll succeed. You have to look at what you want and what your audience wants and then try to determine your probable chances of success.

When should you proceed? When you have a 50-50 chance? A 60-40 chance? An 80-20 chance? *You* have to decide that. Look at the time, energy, and money you'll have to invest to produce and give your presentation. Then decide if the risk is worth the reward.

Just remember–as you become more proficient in making presentations, the risk/reward ratio will begin to shift in your favor.

Don't Say "Yes" Unless . . .

Most people are flattered when asked to make a presentation.

Advertising executive Ron Hoff used to be and would usually accept with only a perfunctory question or two.

But no more. Now Ron is cautious. He asks plenty of questions before accepting an invitation to speak. And he advises other people to do the same.

The change in Ron's *modus operandi* came about, as he explained in an article in *Advertising Age,* after he was invited to make a presentation to an advertising club in a midwestern city. He accepted, prepared his talk, then flew from New York to the engagement. When the time came for Ron to speak, he stepped to the platform and looked out on an audience of five people.

"Never again," Ron says. Now he requires answers to a number of questions before he agrees to give a talk. He suggests all speakers and presenters do the same.

Ron asks for all pertinent information such as dates, time, the proposed subject, and the makeup of the audience (which, when provided, gives you a running start on compiling your audience profile). He also asks for information on how the presentation will be promoted and publicized (important not only to you but also to the organization you represent). Ron makes about 10 presentations a year, so he also asks about the financial arrangements–who is to pay for transportation, meals, and lodging? Finally, he asks if the organizer of the event is assured of an audience and of what size. He doesn't want to talk to a handful of strangers again.

Other experienced speakers suggest additional questions to be added to Ron's basic list:

- What type of talk is expected? Factual, humorous, inspirational?
- Who will be handling the arrangements and where can this person be reached (at home, office, or club)?
- What kind of clothing is appropriate? Is the occasion for your presentation formal, business, informal?
- What is the schedule of events on the day of your presentation? Will you be speaking in the morning, afternoon, or evening? First, second, or last on the program?
- What is the physical setup at the presentation site? Will you be at a podium? Will there be room and electrical facilities for projectors and screen? Are there lights or other obstructions that may prevent effective projection?

Once you have answers to these questions, and have set your objectives and analyzed your audience, you can say "yes" or "no" to an invitation with a firm conviction that you have made a well-considered decision.

communication objectives, we'll refer to them as production requirements.

Many presenters, if they bother to perform preproduction analysis at all, start with the second set of objectives, the production requirements. When asked to make a presentation or when they seek a forum for their ideas, they immediately start thinking about their production requirements. They decide "to give a 20-minute talk." Or "to make a slide presentation." Or "to use film along with my talk." This sort of decision-making is putting the cart before the horse. It's not very productive to decide how you're going to put a presentation together until you know exactly what you hope to accomplish.

Start With a "Behavior Change"

You have to start with the statements of your communication objectives. Since these are statements of the audience responses you hope to stimulate, you should think of your *communications objectives as statements of behavior changes.* What sort of behavior changes do you want to produce in your audience? Do you want them to feel differently? Think differently? Act differently?

When you're satisfied you have an answer to those questions, phrase that answer in a statement that contains an infinitive verb phrase. For example, if you're a market development manager planning a presentation for a sales convention, your statement might contain the phrases "to generate enthusiasm for our new line of products" or "to trigger orders for our products." If you're a candidate for political office, your statement would probably read "to convince people to vote for me." If you're a concerned citizen making a presentation to government officials, your statement might read "to persuade listeners to act on my concerns."

A presenter must consider the motivations of an audience.

Once you've established your *communications* objective (or objectives if you want your presentation to create more than a single response), your next step is to analyze your *audience's* objectives. You need to determine what will motivate them to listen to you and, more importantly, what will lead them to respond in the ways you desire.

This determination is going to require detailed audience analysis. You have to develop a general profile of your audience. Some of the material for this profile will be relatively easy to discover. It's the objective data: average age, sex, current profession (if important), educational and skill-training background, and so on. This information will tell you *who* your audience is. The other material you'll need—the more important material—will require a little more analysis and extrapolation on your part. If you're to be successful in creating a change in audience behavior, you have to know what motivates the average audience member. That means asking yourself (or, if possible, surveying a representative sample of people from the probable audience) two general questions:

Why are these people willing to come to my presentation?

What do they hope to gain from what I say?

Let's tie these questions back to the examples used to illustrate the formation of communications objectives. When a market development manager analyzes the probable makeup of an audience at a sales convention, he or she is going to discover, not surprisingly, that the audience will be made up of sales reps, dealers, and distributors for the company's products. Looking into the motivations of these people, the manager would probably discover that most of the people have attended for economic reasons: Their livelihood is tied to what the manager has to say. And what do they hope to gain? Demonstration that the manager's new products can improve their sales more than another manufacturer's products. Successful political candidates probably know the makeup of their constituency as well as they know their own families, but they still have to give some thought to what audiences hope to gain from their presentations. Do the voters want assurance or do they

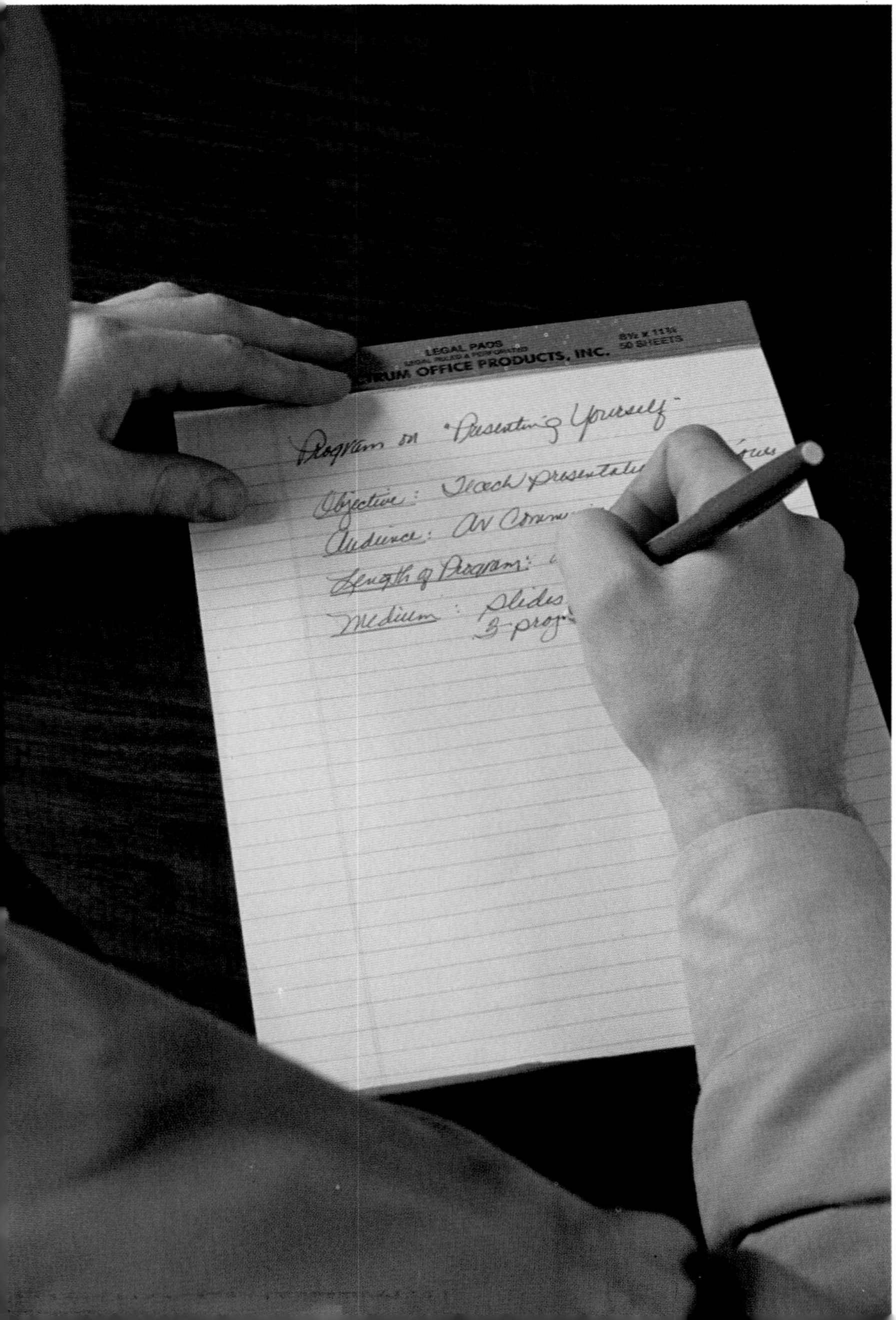

want change? Do they want lower taxes or increased services? Do they want lower inflation or more rapid business expansion? The answers to these questions are as important as what the candidate wants to say.

Taking Aim on Your Target

Once you've established your communications objectives and analyzed the background and motivations of your probable audience, you're ready to determine your presentation requirements. If you enjoy puzzles and mind-challenging games, this is where the fun of preparation comes in. You have your objectives, and you know what themes and appeals are likely to motivate your audience. So how do you tailor your message to match your objectives? How do you deliver your message? What's the optimum length for your presentation? Should you use questions and answers at the end? Will slides work more effectively than motion pictures? Or maybe both together in a multi-image presentation would be more effective?

The list of questions can and should go on until you're satisfied you've found the most effective means of creating the desired behavior change in your audience.

Bear in mind, there are no "right" answers to these questions. The themes, media, and approach you develop for one audience won't necessarily work as effectively with another. As a review of automotive advertising shows us, some people buy cars because of fuel economy, some because of styling, some because of cost (whether it's low or high). If you were to make a presentation to these people, you would have to adapt your message and media to these different motivations–even though your overall communications objective would remain the same.

So rather than look for the "right" combination of presentation requirements–or the "acceptable" or "common" combination–you must look for the most effective combination of message, media, and methods for that particular audience. Remember, you're trying to "engineer" a change in your audience, so you have to start with that change and work back. How can you take an audience whose motivations you know and change their way of thinking, feeling, or acting to yours? When you can answer that question, you'll be finished with your preliminary planning.

Just What Do You Mean?

If you were to tell the chairmen of several manufacturing companies that "profits are the lifeblood of industrial development," would they understand what you meant?

If you said the same thing to assembly-line workers, would they take away the same meaning?

Probably not. And that points out one of the hazards of communication: It isn't enough to say what you mean. You have to say what you mean in a way that ties into the experience of your listeners. If you don't, you're just talking, not communicating.

Linguists call this process of meaning-making on the part of a listener or viewer *transderivational search.* What this lengthy term means is that words (or visual symbols) call into the consciousness of the receiver certain parts of his or her experience, while leaving out others. Another way of putting this is that each of us sees and hears from our past. If our past includes positive associations with such words as "profits" and "industrial development," we would tend to understand–comprehend–the above statement. But if our past includes negative associations–low wages, high prices, strikes, poor-quality merchandise–we would tend not to understand the statement the way it is intended.

In preparing a presentation, you should be aware of the process of transderivational search. You should understand that what you mean and what you say must tie into the experience and motivations of your listeners.

One way to do this, linguists tell us, is to be as concrete and specific as possible. If, for example, we want to make our meaning clear to assembly-line workers, we should not use the words "profits" and "industrial development." Instead, we should talk about "the money we had left after paying our bills to buy new equipment for you to use." That brings the statement into the experience, and in line with the motivations, of the assembly-line workers.

(Please note: This isn't talking *down* to a listener; it's talking *to* a listener.)

Another effective way to tie your meaning into the experience of your audience is to use visuals, such as slides or film. Visuals, by their very nature, are concrete. They show; they tie directly into what the viewer has already experienced. So instead of talking about "profits" or "the equipment you use," you can simply say, "Here's where our money goes," then show slides or film of manufacturing equipment being used by the assembly-line workers. If the statement is true (and it must be if you are to be a creditable communicator), and if the visuals show new equipment in use, you've tied your meaning into the audience's experience.

You've communicated what you "mean."

The more you understand your audience, the greater your chances of getting your message across.

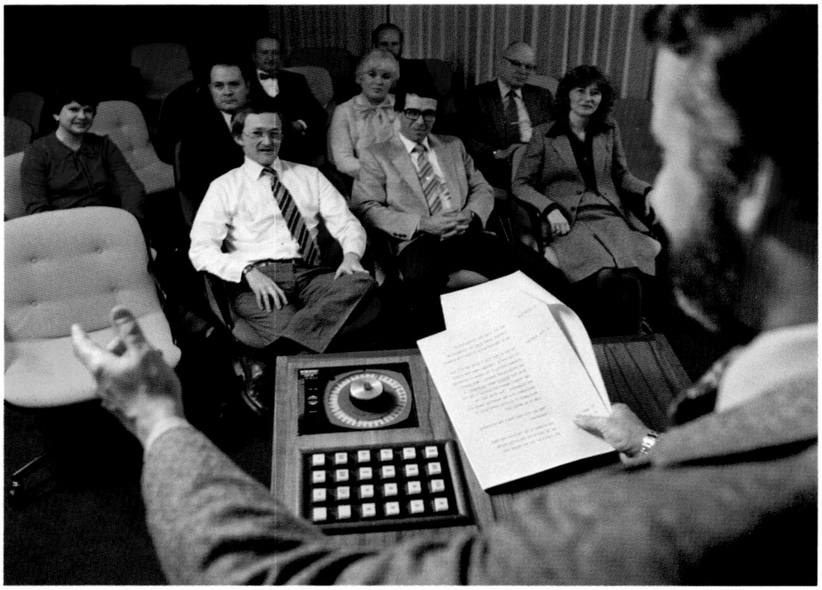

This is the sort of analysis and planning that Ed, Martha, and Robert *didn't do* when they created and gave their presentations.

Ed didn't look deeply enough into the backgrounds of his audience. If he had, he would have scaled down his examples to a level consistent with the motivating needs of his listeners.

Martha didn't analyze the background or motivations of her audience members. If she had, she would have discovered that the women in her audience had already achieved success in the business world. Their motivation–the benefit they hoped to gain–was to learn what they have to do to move from middle management to upper management positions. Knowing this, Martha could have changed the thrust of her talk from overcoming stereotypes to strategies for demonstrating high-level competence.

Robert also failed to analyze the background of his audience. He didn't determine that business and government leaders come to presentations to get the facts and figures they need to make decisions. He also failed to determine that these people are usually pressed for time. So he gave them a long presentation of impressions, just the sort of presentation guaranteed to annoy and anger them. Had he used his multi-image techniques and programming to create interesting, fact-filled information displays, he would have stood a much greater chance of gaining his objective.

If all of this analysis and planning sounds manipulative, you're right. But there's nothing inherently wrong with that. After all, isn't that the intent of most communication, whether the intent has been consciously formed or not? We usually want to gain something from people when we talk with them, even if that gain is little more than a brief smile signaling acceptance. Usually, however, we're looking for more. We may be seeking approval or agreement; we may be trying to persuade and convince; or we may be trying to impress.

So developing a presentation in light of an audience's motivations is indeed a calculated attempt to achieve your objectives. And the truth is, the more you understand and appreciate that point, the better a communicator you'll become.

Worksheet 1 Setting Your Objectives

This work sheet will help you launch your preparation.

Occasion

Possible theme or topic

Communications objective (e.g., What I want to gain from this presentation)

"to "

Audience analysis (general background):	Age:
	Sex:
	Business or profession:
	Education or training:
	Other pertinent information:
Audience analysis (motivation):	Why are audience members willing to come to my presentation?
	What do they hope to gain from what I have to say?
Planning decisions:	Knowing my audience's background and motivations, what's the most effective way to achieve my objectives?
	How should I refine my topic and theme?
	How can I tailor my message?
	What examples or illustrations can be most effective?
	What media can I use?
	How long should my presentation run?

Types of Presentations

Two communication specialists from the same company are asked to prepare presentations.

Ann is asked to prepare a presentation for security analysts who will meet with her company's chief executive officer in the company's boardroom.

Bill is asked to prepare a presentation for the annual meeting of shareholders. It too will be given by the CEO, only he will be addressing 2,000 people in an auditorium rented for the occasion.

Both Ann and Bill will be working with the same content–facts and figures relating to the company's past, current, and future performance. But neither will prepare in the same way. Even though they both work for the same company and are both preparing presentations dealing with identical subject matter, their presentations will be radically different.

The reason for their different approaches is this: Presentations are custom-designed performances. Their length, their overall structure, the media, and equipment used, even the method of delivery used by the presenter are determined by very specific

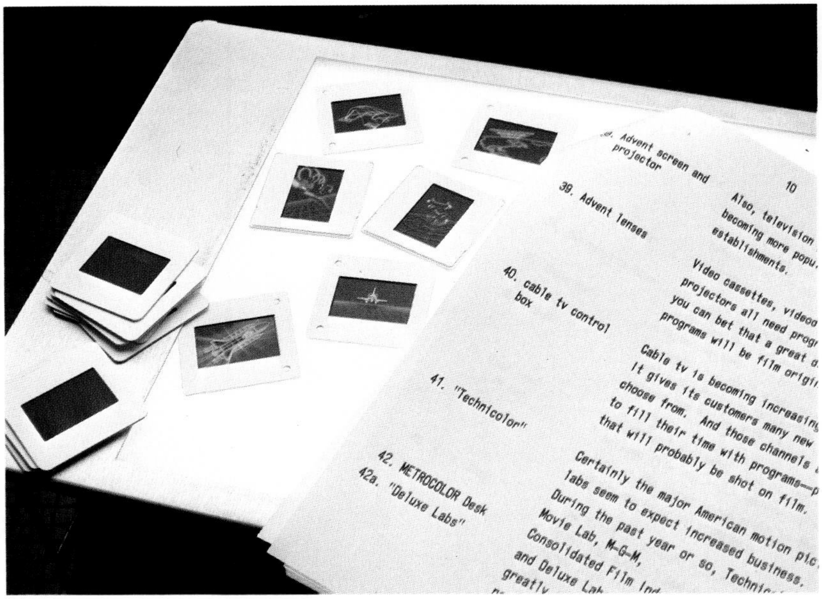

requirements, requirements set by the nature of the presentation.

In our examples above, the nature of the presentation being planned by Ann can be characterized as a statistical profile for a small group of sophisticated, informed, and objective listeners. Facts and figures will dominate this presentation, which will be held in an intimate setting to create an atmosphere of open communication and trust. The visual portion of the presentation will be businesslike, using clear and concise graphics, informative photography, and conservative production techniques. Ann's goal is to influence the opinions and judgments of the analysts with *information* relevant to the company's financial prospects.

The nature of Bill's presentation is entirely different. It can be characterized as a public relations promotion of corporate achievements, given to a large group of subjectively interested, moderately informed listeners. Although the same facts and figures used in Ann's presentation can be used here, they will receive less emphasis. Instead, the presentation will concentrate on the factors that contribute to those figures—people, products, marketing plans, research developments. A large screen and large images—multi-images—will be used to present this information because the purpose of this presentation is more than to just document achievements; it's also intended to create the *impression* of success—continuing, inevitable success. Bill wants to assure—or persuade—shareholders that they're correct in placing continued confidence in the company.

These are only some of the differences between the two presentations; there are many more, some equally as important as those mentioned. But the purpose of this section is not to analyze these hypothetical presentations in depth. Rather, it is to give you the background necessary to analyze the presentation *you're* preparing for.

As mentioned above, each presentation is, in a very real sense, a custom-designed performance, so each will present you with a different set of requirements to consider in planning. But although each presentation is different, it is possible to make some general observations about the different types of presentations.

For the purposes of this section, we've divided presentations into eight different types. We've analyzed each type in terms of purpose, typical audience, production considerations, and special approaches to preparations. We've also examined the advantages and disadvantages of each type. Finally, for each category we've presented a case history showing how an organization has used the presentation type to solve a communication problem.

Of course, as you read these descriptions, you'll see that the classifications are not mutually exclusive. Overlapping does exist. There may even be special categories of presentations that we've overlooked.

So don't use the following descriptions as conclusive explanations of the types of presentations. They're not. And they're not meant to be. At best, they're general planning guidelines—ideas and considerations to mull over as you launch your own preparations.

Sales—Person-to-Person, or Person-to-Small Group

Purpose

The purpose of this type of presentation is to convince an individual or a small group of individuals to buy a product or service, or to entertain further proposals or demonstrations that will lead to the purchase of a product or service.

Audience

The audience for this type of presentation generally consists of a potential buyer or buyers from an industrial company, retail store, or government agency. These people are typically professional buyers, accustomed to evaluating the products and proposals of a large number of sellers. In some cases, these people may spend several hours a day listening to sales presentations.

The motivation of typical audience members is uncomplicated: They want to gather the information they need to make prudent purchasing decisions. This means they're more favorably impressed by a no-nonsense, fact-filled presentation, one that gives them prices, features, benefits, and other pertinent information in a logical, concise fashion.

Production Considerations

1. Setting. This sort of presentation is usually given in a buyer's office or in a small conference room set aside for sales presentations; in most cases this room is not equipped for major audio-visual presentations.

2. Seating. No formal seating pattern exists. Audience members sit either behind a desk or around a small conference table. The presenter must find a spot within this arrangement where he or she can dominate attention.

3. Equipment. The most practical unit for this type of presentation is a desk-top, self-contained projector. Projector, screen, and audio playback equipment are built right into these units, thus reducing the amount of equipment a presenter must carry and simplifying setup time. In most cases, to get ready, a presenter only has to plug in the unit.

Of course, if the presentation is to take place in the office of the presenter, the equipment to be used can be as varied and sophisticated as the presenter's budget and skills allow.

4. Media. Two-inch-by-two-inch slides are the most popular medium for this type of presentation. In presentations where motion is essential to convey information, super 8 or 16 mm sound film is the medium usually chosen.

If the narration accompanying the visual presentation is to be "canned," the audio is usually recorded on a tape cassette, which is played back using the desk top unit's built-in equipment.

5. Length. Because this type of presentation is meant either to introduce or to reinforce the sales representative's oral presentation, and because the typical audience member will be pressed for time, it's wise to keep this type of presentation between 5 and 10 minutes long. If you're considering a longer presentation, make sure you have a valid reason for doing so. In most cases, tighter editing can shorten a presentation so that it won't exceed the 10-minute limit.

6. Assistants. This type of presentation usually requires no assistance.

Preparation

One of the most effective ways of using this type of presentation is to make it a complete presentation in itself, one that can be "plugged in" to a sales rep's overall presentation. For example, a sales rep can make a few preliminary remarks,

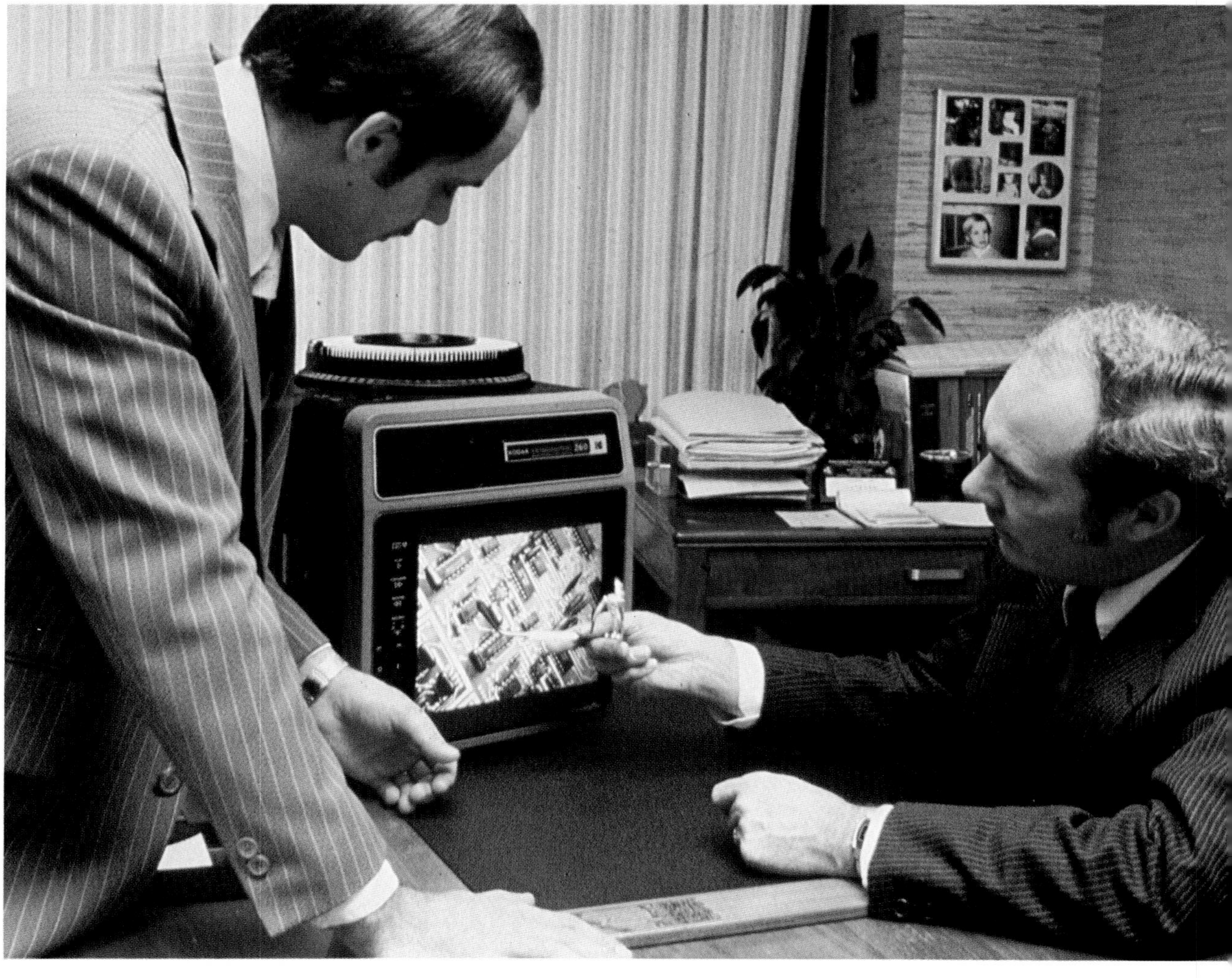

A person-to-person sales presentation
must be fact-filled and to-the-point.

perhaps stating a problem that may be facing members of the audience. Following that, the sales rep runs the audiovisual portion of the presentation to *demonstrate* how and why the product can help solve the problem. The sales rep then takes center stage again to close the presentation–and the sale.

This sort of approach requires that a full script of the visual presentation be written and recorded. Visuals should be shot and programmed to achieve the emphasis indicated by the script. The presenter's introductory and follow-up remarks should also be written beforehand. The main points of this material should be memorized by the sales rep. This portion of the presentation should sound smooth and polished, but not overrehearsed. A presentation that sounds too mechanical may turn off audience members.

Analysis

1. Advantages. This type of presentation is easy and inexpensive to produce and extremely portable and convenient to use, no matter what the setting. If produced as a slide presentation, it will be easy to update and to adapt-an important consideration if the presenter will be calling on customers with different categories of needs. If a taped narration is used with the visuals, the presentation is also "accurate and repeatable"–key information is presented each time with the exact words, figures, and emphasis desired by the presenter.

2. Disadvantages. Creatively, there's only so much you can do with a presentation produced for desk-top projection equipment, especially if your medium is slides. The screens in these units are small, and slide changes come one at a time with a momentary lapse between each change. So don't think about this type of presentation in terms of visual pyrotechnics; it's just not in the nature of the medium. This is a just-the-facts-type of presentation. No thrills, no frills. But extremely effective in presenting facts and figures.

Case History

Bobbie Brooks, Inc., is a leading designer and manufacturer of women's apparel, which it sells to department stores and speciality shops throughout the United States. In the past the company's sales reps called on buyers carrying portable racks of new fashions and portfolios of photographs showing models wearing the clothing. In some cases, actual models were taken along to stage a small-scale fashion show. Needless to say, these presentations were time-consuming and costly, especially since the sales reps would make up to six presentations a year to their top customers.

To reduce its presentation costs and to eliminate complex logistics, Bobbie Brooks decided to build its presentations around a desk-top audiovisual unit. Using slides shot by professional fashion photographers and a sophisticated sound-and-music audio track, the company created a presentation that sells. Each buyer gets to see the company's apparel modeled by such stars as Suzanne Sommers and Cheryl Tiegs, something that would have been impossible in the past. In addition, say the company's marketing people, the narration is done precisely the way they want it, and it's backed by music selected to create "just the right mood" for the clothing being exhibited.

Sales—Point of Purchase

Purpose

To convince a consumer to buy the product being demonstrated.

Audience

Consumers. Typical audience members for this type of presentation are shoppers walking through a store. They may not initially even be interested in the product being demonstrated. The presentation is designed to attract attention to the product and emphasize its appeal.

The motivations of typical audience members are those usually associated with consumer purchases—the desire to gain health, time, popularity, praise, prestige, success, comfort, leisure, security. If a presentation appeals to one of these motives, it can catch the attention and interest of most consumers.

Production Considerations

1. Setting. In almost all cases this type of presentation is made in a retail sales area. Often the demonstration area is the focal point of a larger product display. In some cases, a salesperson plays an integral part in the presentation; in other cases, the "canned" presentation carries the principal sales message, with the sales clerk serving as a source of additional information.

2. Seating. No formal arrangement. Interested consumers usually gather around the presentation area.

3. Equipment. Here again, a desk-top unit—whether for slides, filmstrips, or super 8 film—can be used. Its compact size and ease of operation make it a practical choice for this type of presentation.

4. Media. The media most commonly used include slides, super 8 film, and filmstrips. In almost all cases, a narrated audio track is also used with the presentation.

5. Length. Shoppers are usually people in a hurry. That means a presentation has to grab their attention, make its appeal, and urge a decision to buy in a short period of time. People will watch a presentation "on impulse" for a while, but don't expect them to devote 10 minutes or more. Most professionals try to tell their story in 1 to 3 minutes.

6. Assistants. None required for most portable units.

Preparation

Because the key selling themes are contained in the "canned" audiovisual presentation, a full script must be written and recorded. A storyboard or similar visual planning device should be used to develop the slide or film sequences.

Because most of these presentations are used by retail personnel, a producer should also supply supplemental information such as a product fact sheet, an explanation of the purpose of the presentation, instructions for operating projection equipment, and perhaps a sheet of commonly asked questions (with suggested answers). The salesperson should become familiar with this material, but there's no need to rehearse any formal presentation. In this type of presentation, the salesperson serves as an adjunct to the prepared material.

Analysis

1. Advantages. A point-of-purchase presentation is an extremely effective and inexpensive way to attract consumers to new products (as was the case when fish-line lawn trimmers were first introduced), to expen-

In a point-of-purchase presentation, the theme must be stated quickly and emphatically to attract an audience.

sive products (such as automobiles, motorcycles, and houses), and to products whose appeal may not be readily apparent to consumers. (One company uses point-of-purchase presentations to demonstrate the excellent qualities of its paint products over those of its numerous competitors.)

Point-of-purchase presentations are also an extremely reliable method of presenting a sales message. The basic selling story is contained in the audio and visual elements of the "canned" presentation, where they can be repeated with accuracy and emphasis at every showing. Thus the chances of a poor presentation caused by the lack of skill of a live presenter are reduced to a minimum.

2. Disadvantages. Of all the different types of presentations, this is perhaps the most mechanical. Unlike the previous type of presentation, where the audiovisual element was used to support and reemphasize what a live presenter had to say, a point-of-purchase presentation is usually used to substitute for a live presenter. Of course, the reasons for this substitution may be valid. Often, as is the case in realty offices and new car showrooms, point-of-purchase presentations are used to presell prospects by explaining and illustrating the different buying options available. This approach allows salespeople to concentrate more of their efforts on actual selling.

In other cases, point-of-purchase demonstrations are used because skilled presenters just aren't available, or because they don't have the experience to carry the responsibility of a presentation alone. This is often the case in retail stores.

But some people aren't persuaded by point-of-purchase presentations, especially those that are totally "canned." Because they lack human involvement, these presentations are often seen as nothing more than a television commercial moved into a store. Keep this consideration in mind when planning for a presentation. If you believe your product or service needs the involvement of a salesperson to close the sale, consider using a person-to-person sales presentation. If your product can sell itself and you can limit the involvement of a salesperson to answering questions and writing up an order, a point-of-purchase presentation may be all you need.

Case History

If you walk into a sporting goods store or the sporting goods department of a major store, you'll find it hard to believe that people need—or even want— another game to play.

That was the situation facing Jokari/U.S.A., Inc., when it sought to introduce its new racquet-ball-on-a-string game to American consumers. In fact, the problem Jokari faced was twofold: Not only was its game new, but to demonstrate its appeal physically they needed an extensive area and the talents of two skilled players.

Jokari solved this problem by producing a film demonstrating the simplicity and appeal of the game. A match between two skilled players was filmed on 16 mm film, then reduced for super 8 use with compact tabletop viewers. The viewers were placed in major retail outlets throughout the country. In addition to the media, Jokari provided program instructions and recommendations, so salespeople could become effective elements of the point-of-purchase demonstration. According to company officials, this approach produced sales that far exceeded their expectations.

General Sales Meeting

Purpose

The purpose of a general sales meeting differs with the type of audience. If aimed at sales representatives, its purpose is (1) to inform the audience members of new products, services, pricing schedules, and sales and advertising plans; (2) to generate enthusiasm for the new products and plans; and (3) to motivate audience members to increase their sales. If aimed at customers, the purpose of a general sales meeting is (1) to generate interest in the presenter's products and (2) to pave the way for a subsequent call by a sales rep.

Audience

General sales meetings are of two types: the first involves communication from key executives in a marketing or sales department to sales representatives, distributors, or dealers; the second involves communication from marketing or sales representatives to executives or buyers from major accounts.

Naturally, the motivation of the audience groups is different. Sales reps, dealers, and distributors want to increase their sales; they're motivated by the possibility of professional success and financial gain. Customers and prospects seek solutions to actual or potential problems; they're motivated by the need to maintain or gain competence in their fields.

Production Considerations

1. Setting. Because this type of presentation is typically made to a large audience, considerable room is required. Some companies rent local movie or stage theatres for an afternoon or evening and hold their meetings there. Others rent hotel ballrooms, convention halls, or the auditorium of a local school. In short, general sales meetings usually require enough room to seat up to several hundred people.

2. Seating. When dealing with this many people, theatre-style seating is the only feasible arrangement. If the presentation is to be given in an auditorium or theatre, the seating problem all but resolves itself. The only additional work may involve the elimination of marginal seating. If the presentation is to be given in a ballroom or convention hall, folding chairs must be brought in and arranged in a suitable seating pattern. See page 166 for suggestions for setting up theatre-style seating.

3. Equipment. The type of presentation to be given will determine the specific units of equipment required. For the purpose of planning, this equipment can be divided into three groups: (1) projection equipment–one or more projectors (slide or motion picture), dissolve controls, a programmer, (2) audio equipment–tape playback unit, amplifiers, speakers, microphones, and (3) screens–screen or screens capable of providing a sharp, bright image to viewers throughout the seating area.

Many sales meetings are extremely elaborate, often taking on the appearance of a stage show. They use equipment such as spotlights, laser displays, turntable stages, fountains, and the specialized microphones and audio equipment needed to carry the performances of singers and a live orchestra. All this costs money, of course, but more important, it requires the talents of specialists. If you're thinking of developing a presentation of this type, find a specialist who can handle your equipment needs.

General sales meetings usually require considerable room and planning.

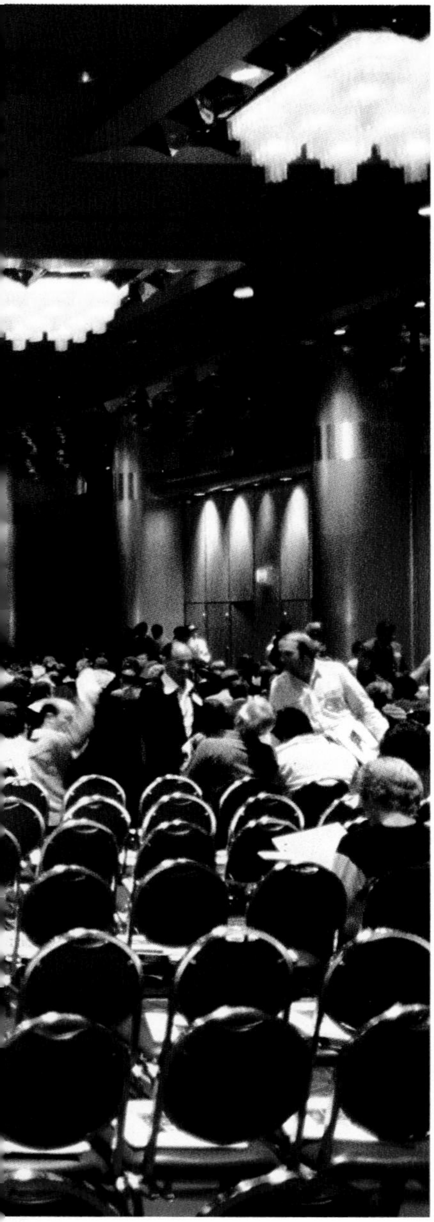

4. Media. The medium used most often for this type of presentation is the 2-by-2-inch slide. In many cases, 16 mm motion pictures also are used in conjunction with the slides. (Where the projection distance is great, some producers prefer to use 35 mm motion picture sequences to equalize the brightness of the slide and film images.)

In sales presentations, most–if not all–of the narration is delivered by a presenter or presenters. Some presentations do use audiotape, however, to carry key interviews, music, sound effects, or other special audio material.

5. Length. It's hard to pin down the length of this type of presentation. Most run at least a half hour; the average time is probably in the 45-to-60-minute range; some, however, run for several hours or more. A presentation of this length is usually broken up into several smaller presentations to avoid the problem of audience fatigue. (See page 112 for a discussion of presentation length.) A general observation can be made about the length of a presentation and the demands it places on the presenter: The more show, the more of a showman or showwoman needed. Only an experienced and talented presenter (aided by an experienced and talented producer) can keep an audience alert and interested for more than 30 to 45 minutes. If you're thinking of a presentation in this time range–or beyond it–consider hiring a professional presentation producer.

6. Assistants. The larger, the longer, and the more elaborate the presentation, the greater the need for assistants. For a general sales meeting, assistants are usually needed to write the script, prepare the slides, program the visual sequences, select and set up the equipment, and operate the equipment while the presenter is speaking on stage. And, of course, as the presentation becomes more sophisticated, so does the need for more specialized assistants. If, for example, you're planning to use spotlights to focus attention on a number of presenters, you may find you need a lighting director to plan this aspect of the presentation, as well as a specialist to operate the lights on the day of the performance.

Preparation

Extensive preparation is a must for this type of presentation. A scriptwriter is needed to prepare the narrative portion of the presentation. This writer must be able to plan for not only the content of the presentation, but also for the dramatic effect to be created on the stage and the screen. Similarly, an experienced photographer, director, and producer will be required to create the visual elements and to program all elements of the presentation. If audiotape will be used in the presentation, sound specialists and a recording and mixing studio will be needed.

The on-stage presenter also will find that more time must be given to preparation. Since in this type of presentation visual changes are tied to the speaker's words, the presenter will read his or her words from a prepared text. A considerable amount of rehearsal is usually needed to polish the presenter's delivery so that emphasis and pauses come at just the right points. Rehearsal will also be needed to polish the interaction between presenter and visuals. Projectionists will have to familiarize themselves with the presenter's pace of delivery, just as the presenter will have to familiarize himself or herself with the pacing of the visual sequences.

Analysis

1. Advantages. The effectiveness of this type of presentation can be as controlled and emphatic as a Broadway stage play. Nothing is left to chance or to improvisation. Every word and visual, as well as the interaction between the two, is planned—and delivered as planned. The result is impact.

2. Disadvantages. Naturally this type of presentation is costly, in terms of both time and money. Hundreds of hours may be required to plan and present a general sales meeting, and the cost for this effort can run from $10,000 to more than $100,000 for major all-day presentations. This money, however, may be well spent. Recently, for example, a major manufacturer of audiovisual equipment put on an elaborate sales presentation that carried a budget-draining price tag. But when the company's leading marketing executive was asked if the presentation was worth the cost, he answered with an emphatic *yes*. Aided in large part by the presentation, the company had taken equipment orders whose value far exceeded the cost of the show.

Case History

Datsun, like other car manufacturers, has a sales training problem. Its success depends on the efforts of an informed and dedicated sales force. But the sales force doesn't work for the company. It works for the hundreds of independent dealers who carry Datsun's line of cars and trucks.

That means if Datsun made no effort of its own, the company's sales would hinge on the training and motivational efforts of its dealers. That's a big risk for a car manufacturer to take. It can't assume that every dealership will have people skilled in sales training and motivation. Nor can it assume that each dealer will emphasize the key points Datsun feels are important to sell its cars.

To overcome this problem, Datsun relies on major presentations—made not only to dealers but also to dealer sales forces. The purpose of these presentations is to

Dazzling effects on the screen reflect the extensive preparation that went into Datsun's new car announcement presentation.

teach the salespeople the features and benefits of the company's new line of cars and trucks. The presentations also build enthusiasm, leaving the salespeople eager to sell the Datsun line.

The Datsun 1982 new car announcement presentation was produced by Chris Korody, president of Image Stream, a media production company based in Los Angeles. The hour-long presentation was shown in 39 cities throughout the United States. More than 6,500 Datsun salespeople saw the presentation.

It may be more accurate to say "participated in the presentation."

"No one wants to sit through an hour-long instructional presentation," says Korody. "So we sugarcoated it. The presentation was structured around a rally, with each of seven car models leaving from different points around the United States in a race to Salina, Kansas, the geographical center of the country."

To create immediate involvement and interest in the presentation, the salespeople "bet" on which rally team would win the race. After that, the main segments of the presentation were given.

The presentation consisted of a series of training modules. Each module presented information on the features and selling points of a particular model of the new Datsun. This information was presented through multi-image presentations, clips from the company's new advertising campaign, and 16 mm motion picture film vignettes showing the cars participating in the rally. In total, Korody estimates the presentation used about 35 minutes of multi-image and about 25 minutes of 16 mm film. The multi-image portion of the presentation consisted of a 15-projector, 2,850-slide production, that was shown on a special wide screen.

After each pair of modules, the Datsun sales training team presenting the show conducted product knowledge games to reinforce the audience's retention of information. Prizes were awarded to the people with the most correct answers.

Korody admits that the rally and the contests were gimmicks. "But," he adds, "they were necessary. A lot of the features we talked about were common to a number of cars, but that didn't mean we could just overlook a feature the second or third time we came to it. We had to present this information every time. We used the contest-like atmosphere as a different way to ensure audience involvement and to reinforce the product information."

The presentation was shown during October 1981, to coincide with the public introduction of the 1982 Datsun cars and trucks. Three presentation crews–each consisting of technical specialists from Staging Techniques and sales trainers from Datsun–put on an average of nine presentations a week. Audience size ranged from as few as 50 to more than 250 salespeople.

Five trucks were needed to transport sets, screens, and projection equipment from city to city to meet the 30-day schedule. Staging Techniques' Los Angeles office provided all equipment, built the sets, and handled logistics for the presentation.

Workshops

Purpose

To impart knowledge or skills. Some workshops are meant only to convey information, which participants need to perform their jobs more effectively. Such is the case when a workshop examining the features and benefits of a new product is conducted for sales representatives. The more common type of workshop concentrates on skill training.

Audience

Generally speaking, a person attending a workshop is someone who needs information or training. Beyond this description, however, it's difficult to generalize about audience members. Some may bring general education skills to a workshop, while others, such as engineers and scientists, often attend workshops to learn about new products and techniques that can help them in their work.

For the most part, audiences for workshops are highly motivated. They are in attendance because they want the training. A presenter doesn't have to spend much time gaining attention and building interest.

Production Considerations

1. Setting. Workshops are usually given in classrooms, lecture halls, or laboratories where participants can practice skills being taught. These settings must contain adequate seating for the participants, appropriate training equipment, and audiovisual equipment.

2. Seating. Seating patterns for this type of presentation are of two sorts. If the audience is large and if there are no demonstrations the participants must view at close range, lecture hall seating is adequate, with chairs or desks arranged in a conventional pattern of rows and aisles. If the audience is small, or if there are demonstrations to be observed, seating arrangements such as those illustrated on page 167 are more effective for a workshop. These types of seating patterns establish a more intimate relationship between presenter and participants. They also make it easier for participants to view materials and procedures demonstrated by the workshop leader.

3. Equipment. There are no limits on the equipment a workshop leader can select to use with his or her presentation. Desk-top viewers are often used to supplement the workshop leader's presentation. In fact, some workshops use a number of desk-top units programmed to use self-instruction sequences. Conventional slide presentations and 16 mm motion pictures have, of course, been used in education and training for decades, and their use continues despite the inroads made by videotape technology. The same is true for that familiar training standby, the overhead projector. Audiotape recording and playback equipment also is used extensively in workshops, especially in conjunction with slide presentations. Some large training departments have built extensively equipped multi-image/multi-media presentation areas in which to conduct their workshops. These areas contain a wide array of presentation equipment, from desk-top projectors to videotape playback equipment, all controlled by sophisticated programmers.

Of course, the equipment for traveling workshops will be limited to what is convenient to carry. This limitation, however, doesn't preclude the use of sophisticated pre-

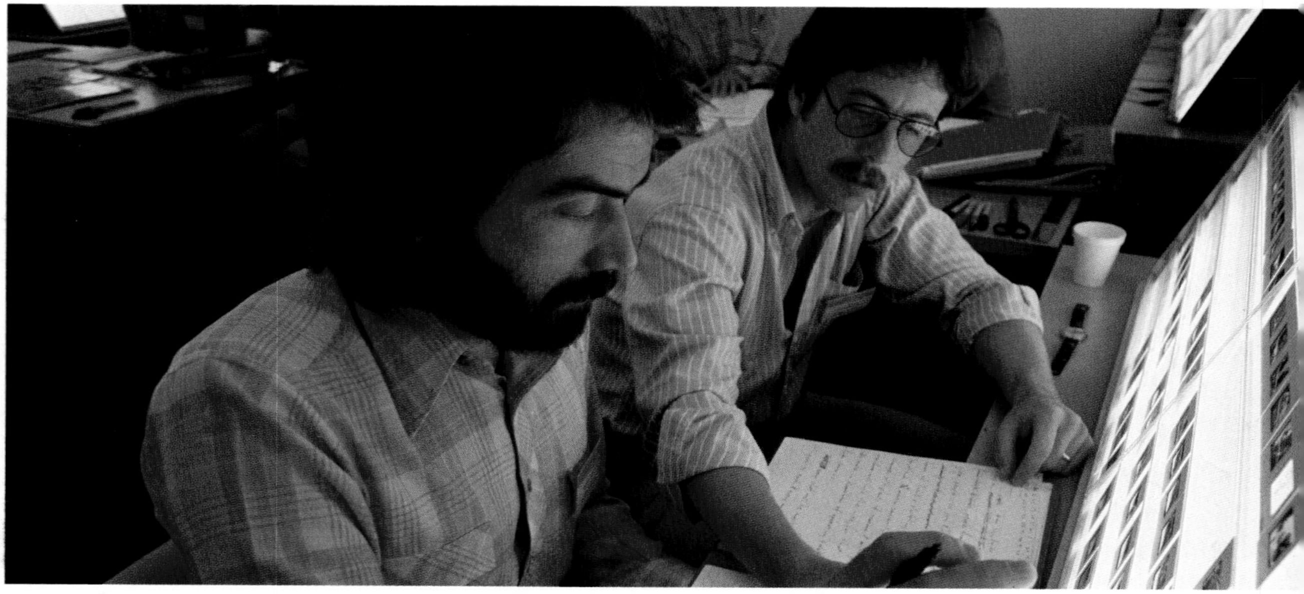

Skill training workshops usually combine formal presentations with hands-on application sessions.

sentations. The equipment for a simple three-projector, multi-image slide presentation, for example, can be contained in a single shipping case.

4. Media. Perhaps the most popular of all the workshop media is the 2-by-2-inch slide. Presentations built around these slides are easy and inexpensive to produce and to change. They're also extremely portable and convenient to use. In many cases, an instructor with only minimum experience in photography can create the slides necessary to illustrate a basic presentation. Transparencies for overhead projection are also easy to prepare and easy to use. Super 8 and 16 mm motion picture films are also popular in workshops, although they usually require more time and money to produce.

5. Length. For the most part, the complexity of the subject matter and the experience and know-how of the participants determines the length of a workshop presentation. Some workshops may cover all pertinent material in 30 minutes or less. Others may require from 3 days to 3 weeks to cover the material to be presented thoroughly. In planning for an extended workshop, be sure to consider the fatigue level of participants. The mind can absorb only so much information at one sitting–and the body can sit still for only so long–so plan adequate breaks and changes of pace. See page 112 for more information on this subject.

6. Assistants. A workshop leader may or may not need an assistant, depending on the complexity of the material being presented. In some presentations, the presenter needs no more than a remote-control unit to advance a slide projector. In others, the presenter may need several assistants to operate projectors and demonstrate procedures. In most cases, common sense will dictate whether or not an assistant is needed.

Preparation

Most workshop leaders, especially those who are thoroughly familiar with their subject matter, prepare extended outlines covering the subject and topics to be covered during their presentations. Only rarely will they write out a full script of their remarks.

That's because a workshop should be based on two-way communication. Effective workshop leaders don't stand before an audience and read instructions. They advance a point, explain it, illustrate or demonstrate it, all the while pacing the presentation on feedback coming from the audience. If the facial expressions and affirmative nods of the audience members tell a presenter the information is being understood, the presenter can continue. But if audience feedback–verbal and nonverbal–indicates that understanding is lacking, the presenter must go back and review the material, often taking a new tack and developing new illustrations and examples. This sort of review can't be written into a script.

If a workshop is to be led by someone without thorough knowledge of the subject matter, a full script of the presentation is usually written. Very often this script will be supplemented with extensive background information. But even here, the presenter is not expected to memorize the script word for word. Instead, the presenter is expected to become thoroughly familiar with the content and flow of the presentation.

The goal is to be able to give the presentation with the same spontaneity and ease as an experienced workshop leader. If this isn't possible, the presenter may work from a set of note cards.

Analysis

1. Advantages. The advantages of a workshop employing audiovisual support can be summed up with a single statistic: We learn about 90 percent of what we know through our eyes. If you can show people what you want them to learn, the chances are great that they will retain a good portion of this message. But if you only tell them what they need to know, or if you give them a sheaf of reading material to memorize, the chances are much less that your teaching or training goal can be reached.

2. Disadvantages. It's difficult to find a solid disadvantage of audiovisually supported instruction. The most obvious disadvantage is that of cost–it's naturally more costly to add visuals to what was previously an oral presentation. But that so-called "cost" is often deceiving, representing a very narrow view of what is to be included in the price of instruction. Most workshop leaders find that audiovisuals reduce the amount of time they need to cover a topic. In addition, workshop participants usually learn faster and remember more of the AV-assisted instruction. So if you subtract the time saved by leader and participants, that alone usually offsets the cost of producing a presentation. If you factor in the increased effectiveness of the people trained, the cost savings brought about by AV-assisted workshops are even greater.

Case History

Hanson Industries of Boulder, Colorado, introduced a new line of ski boots using sales clinics/workshops. The company's goal was to demonstrate the advantages of its new boot as well as to motivate sales clerks from sporting goods outlets to be more excited about selling ski equipment in general and Hanson boots in particular. They accomplished this by using a combination of lectures and sound-slide presentations during 1-day workshops.

The presentations were of two types: A three-projector multi-image presentation accompanied by a rock music sound track was used to communicate the excitement of skiing as well as to provide a change of pace from the more technical presentations. The technical presentations stressed techniques to use in fitting and selling Hanson boots. One presentation was almost completely "canned," while the other consisted of a set of slides accompanied by a commentary delivered by a Hanson representative. The presenter worked from an illustrated outline that matched the sequence of slides.

Mass Audience Meetings

Purpose

On the surface, most presentations of this type seek to convey information. Usually, however, there is a more important purpose–to persuade audience members to accept and act on the information presented.

Audience

This is perhaps the most general of all the categories of presentations. It includes presentations ranging from an annual meeting of shareholders, to keynote addresses at conventions, to guidebook-type presentations used at historical sites. This broad spectrum of presentations means a broad spectrum of audiences–too broad to generalize about, with one exception: The audience members bring a strong, motivating interest to the presentation. They are attending the meeting because the presenter or the subject matter is of considerable importance to them.

Production Considerations

1. Setting. Most presentations of this type are given in auditoriums, banquet halls, hotel ballrooms, gymnasiums, or specially built theatres–just about any open area large enough to hold the expected audience. Some large-scale meetings, especially rallies, are often held outdoors.

2. Seating. When a seating plan is used, it almost always follows a theatre seating arrangement. (See information under General Sales Meeting, page 35 for additional details.)

Some presentations, such as those given at rallies, are made before a standing audience. In planning for this type of presentation, an effort should be made to assure that audience members will have a clear view of the presenter and podium. This is often accomplished by using ropes to guide people into an acceptable viewing area.

3. Equipment. This type of presentation demands large screens, projection equipment capable of filling the screens with bright, sharp images, and audio equipment that can fill the presentation area with clear, crisp sound. The decision on specific types of projection equipment depends on the nature of the presentation.

4. Media. As indicated above, you need media that can be seen and heard by a large and perhaps widely scattered audience. Two-by-two-inch slides or 16 mm motion picture film should provide adequate images in most situations.

The choice between slides and motion picture film depends, of course, on the subject matter. Some material is just more suited to slide presentation. At an annual meeting, for example, where the subject matter is financial figures, charts and graphs, slides are the more practical choice. Artwork can be prepared and photographed easily–and changed virtually up to the last minute. The use of overlays and progressive disclosures also can be used to simplify the presentation of even the most complicated financial matter.

By contrast, some material demands motion and the you-are-there ambience of motion picture film to be effective. This could be the case, for example, in a presentation describing a new medical technique. In this situation, audience members would want to see the new technique in use, under actual clinical conditions, so they can observe all details of the procedure. A second-by-second film presentation does this far more effectively than slides.

In other situations, say at a political rally, for example, where the overall objective is to create an emotional reaction in an audience, film is also a more appropriate choice. Its ability to convey emotion is far greater than all but the most sophisticated slide presentations.

5. Length. Presentations of this type should be limited to 30 minutes, 45 minutes at most. If this is impractical–as is often the case in meetings of shareholders–make sure you provide breaks and changes of pace for the audience. Use more than one speaker, or have one speaker followed by an audiovisual presentation, or have the visual presentation switch from slides to film. (See page 112 for more suggestions.)

6. Assistants. For the reasons explained under General Sales Meetings, you should plan to use assistants for this type of presentation.

Mass audience meetings typically attract a strongly motivated audience.

Preparation

As explained in the discussion of General Sales Meetings, preparations should be thorough. Full scripts should be written, storyboards prepared, rehearsals conducted with complete attention to detail. Presenters should be prepared to read their texts, although their readings should be smooth and well rehearsed. If a question-and-answer period is planned at the conclusion of the formal presentation, that segment should also be "rehearsed." (See page 140 on planning for questions and answers.)

Analysis

1. Advantages. Large-scale presentations produce impact. A big hall, a large screen, large images, and a packed house convey an unstated message—this presentation is important. Because of this, people who have ideas or arguments they want to impress on the minds of their audiences usually choose a major forum for their presentations.

2. Disadvantages. The principal disadvantage of this type of presentation is cost. But as explained under General Sales Meetings, this large initial cost may be more than offset by the gains realized from the presentation.

Case History

Maybe it was the appeal of the psychedelic light shows that used to accompany the acid rock bands of the late 1960's.

Maybe it was the phenomenal success of *Beatlemania*, a 2-hour multi-image presentation that uses John, Paul, George, and Ringo look-alikes in performances given against an everchanging backdrop of slides.

Or maybe it's the long lines that snake their way into the elaborate multimedia presentations that have become the most popular attractions at major fairs and exhibitions.

But whatever the reason, the conclusion is obvious: Audiences are attracted to audiovisual presentations that combine information *and* entertainment.

This fact hasn't been lost on enterprising producers and presenters. They've combined an artist's eye for effects and a producer's eye for profits to create a wide variety of new mass audience presentations.

In cities throughout the world, multimedia and multi-image presentations have become substitutes for tour buses. *The Great Toronto Adventure*, for example, has attracted hundreds of thousands of visitors a year since its opening in 1979. It uses more than 3,000 slides and an array of computer-controlled special effects to take its audiences on a 1-hour "tour" of Toronto's neighborhoods.

Some cities even celebrate special events using mass audience presentations. Miami, for example, used 300 performers and a multi-image presentation on a screen measuring 30 feet by 105 feet to celebrate the nation's bicentennial. More than 9,000 people attended each performance.

Educational and cultural exhibits also have begun to use mass audience presentations to attract visitors. The Museum of the City of New York uses multi-images, sound, maps, and artifacts to re-create the history of the city, in a presentation called *The Big Apple*. And at a special presentation at the Lincoln Center in New York City, three 35 mm motion picture-images were projected onto an 80-by-179-foot screen suspended from the front of the Metropolitan Opera House.

The list of examples could go on, with new presentations being added nearly every week.

The growing popularity of mass audience presentations has even led one Los Angeles-based producer to enter into a partnership with a manufacturer of dome theatres. Their goal: To provide the theatre, equipment, and media needed to stage mass audience presentations.

"The idea has just taken hold," says Alan Kozlowski, president of Quantum Leap, Inc., in Venice, California. "You're seeing this type of nontheatrical multimedia presentation in more and more settings—in museums, planetariums, carnivals, theme parks, and of course, business and industrial exhibits."

Kozlowski's initial production in this field is a 12-minute adventure film in the tradition of James Bond. It's called *Sensations*, a title that aptly describes what audiences experience as they're taken on a car chase, a sky dive over the Canadian Rockies, and an underwater chase filmed in the Caribbean. In fact, the audiences are literally enveloped by the film, which is projected onto the interior surface of a dome 70 feet in diameter and about 40 feet high.

The projection system, that was developed by Quantum Leap's Swiss partner, Creative Attractions, uses 70 mm motion picture film. A 46 mm diameter image is contained on each 70 mm frame. The projector is equipped with a 196° lens, raised 6 feet off the floor and aimed straight up into the dome. "The projected image," says Kozlowski, "covers the entire interior surface of the dome down to about 3 feet off the ground."

The presentation has two principal audiences: an admission-paying general audience, who are attracted to the presentation through advertising and promotion; and potential buyers of the presentation concept.

Two types of domes are available, according to Kozlowski, an inflatable model for portable presentations and a geodesic dome for permanent installation. Both hold about 400 people, who stand during the presentation.

In addition to the dome theatre and the projection equipment, which will be supplied by Creative Attractions, buyers will receive filmed presentations. "Initially, we're selling prints of 'Sensations,'" says Kozlowski. "We'll also produce other films for general distribution. A second type of presentation will be those produced for individual clients, whether businesses, government agencies, planetariums, theme parks, or entrepreneurs who want to create a presentation focusing on a community or some other specific theme."

It took Kozlowski about 7 months to produce *Sensations*, including time to create the camera—equipped with a 220° lens—and the special mountings needed to hold the camera during shooting.

For Kozlowski, however, the effort was worth it. When *Sensations* was first shown to audiences at the Oktoberfest festival in Stuttgart, Germany, the response was overwhelming. "There is so much to see and experience in this new medium," he said, "that the number of repeat customers was very high."

Exhibits

Purpose

This could be called a presentation within a presentation. The larger presentation is usually the booth or display set up at a trade show or convention. Within that booth or display, there is usually another presentation, this one featuring a speaker supported by audiovisual material. The purpose of this second presentation is either to attract passersby into the booth, or to present information essential to the presenter's communication goals. This latter purpose makes an exhibit presentation a close kin to the three types of sales-oriented presentations discussed earlier.

Audience

Exhibits are generally of two types: those open to the general public and those open to members of a specific trade group or association. An example of the first type is the auto show exhibition held annually in most major metropolitan areas. This show enables automobile dealers to display their new car lines to the general public. An example of the second type of exhibit is that held in conjunction with the National Audio-Visual Association meeting each year. At this exhibition, manufacturers of audiovisual equipment and suppliers of audiovisual services have the opportunity to display their products to people within the industry.

While most people attending an exhibit are interested in the products and material being displayed, not all can be considered buyers. Many are merely window shoppers, walking by the exhibits out of curiosity or just to kill time. The goal of an exhibit presentation is to turn these browsers into buyers.

Production Considerations

1. Setting. The setting for an exhibit presentation is a booth within a large exhibit hall. In terms of preparations, this means dealing with high ambient light and noise. It also means the possibility of confusion, as members of the audience come and go because their interest waxes or wanes. Because of these factors, preparations must be made to minimize the distractions that may surround the presentation. One way many producers do this is by building a small enclosed theatre within the exhibit area. This allows them to treat the presentation like any other closed-room meeting.

The purpose of an exhibit presentation is to attract and hold the attention of passersby.

Some producers also use beaded screens (see page 107) to limit the viewing area for their presentations. This forces viewers to come within the presentation area, where seats are provided. By keeping viewers within this specific area, the producer gains some control over possible interfering elements.

2. Seating. Seating is usually set up in a theatre pattern; however, the nature of the presentation may eliminate the need for seats. Many presentations are made to standing audiences. This is especially true of presentations made to attract passersby. And many producers use novelty arrangements. Eastman Kodak Company, for example, has used a presentation that required viewers to step up to a counter and look down at images reflected from a mirror-created "pit."

3. Equipment. Here again, the nature of the presentation determines the type of equipment that's most suitable. Theatre-type presentations will require conventional slide or motion picture projectors. Presentations within the exhibit, where the emphasis is on person-to-person selling, may be created around compact desk-top projectors. A high-quality public address system and durable tape playback and amplification equipment are essential for most exhibit presentations. And because these presentations are usually made continuously throughout the day, many producers feel it's also essential to have backup units for all the equipment being used.

4. Media. Any medium or combination of media can be used at an exhibit presentation. Two-by-two-inch slides, filmstrips, super 8 or 16 mm motion picture film, videotape–the choice depends on the nature of the exhibit area and the budget for production. By far the most popular medium is slides–and for the familiar reasons: easy to produce and use, inexpensive, easy to change or replace. Slides offer another major advantage for exhibit presentations: They allow a presenter with a remote-control unit to control the pacing of the presentation. If the presenter sees the audience is losing interest, he or she can pick up the pace until a new subject area renews viewer interest. By the same token, the presenter can dwell a little longer at points that produce deep viewer involvement. This sort of response to audience feedback isn't possible with film or videotape productions.

5. Length. Most exhibit presentations are short. Those used to attract a crowd to a booth or display are usually no longer than 5 minutes. The goal of these presentations is to spark audience interest, to raise interesting questions or possibilities, and then to promise answers within the exhibit area. Presentations used within theatres or theatre-like settings usually run about 10 to 15 minutes. This allows time to get across the presenter's message, but it also recognizes that audience members are usually in a hurry to see other exhibits and are apt to get restless after a 10-to-15-minute sit. Person-to-person sales presentations within the exhibit area are also short, for reasons explained in the section devoted to that type of presentation.

6. Assistants. Theatre-type presentations usually require an assistant, either to operate the projection equipment or to monitor the operation of the equipment. Presentations made with tabletop units are completely controlled by the presenter.

Preparation

Preparations for exhibit presentations are as varied as the different types of presentations that may be used. Theatre-type presentations require preparations similar to those described under General Sales Meetings and Mass Audience Meetings. Preparations for exhibit sales presentations are the same as those for person-to-person or point-of-purchase presentations.

Only one additional factor must be considered. Preparations for exhibit presentations should include the suggestions and assistance of the overall exhibit designer. This person can outline the problems of light, noise, and crowd control the presenter can expect to encounter. He or she also can offer solutions to these problems. These solutions may involve building a separate theatre, using special building materials to block out light and noise, or using elements of the exhibit itself to create the boundaries of the presentation area. Ask for this information at initial planning meetings, and welcome and implement the designer's suggestions. They may well spell the difference between success and failure.

Analysis

1. Advantages. Booths and displays at a general exhibit are like so many candy bars on a shelf. The decision to choose one over another may be made on nothing more than impulse. Considering the amount of money that goes into building and staffing a booth, most companies and organizations seek ways to trigger that impulse. Many use vivacious models, others use giveaways. But over the years most exhibitors have found that lively, exciting presentations are prehaps the best way to draw an interested crowd. An exhibit presentation conveys information; it can attract, inform, and motivate the viewer to want to know more. Having done that, it can prepare the viewer for the main event–the people and materials that form the exhibit booth itself.

2. Disadvantages. Perhaps the greatest disadvantage of an exhibit presentation is that it does require room. And room is usually at a premium at most exhibits. That means the person responsible for the exhibit is going to have to trade some selling room for a presentation area. Of course, a presentation does contribute to the selling effort, so the trade-off may not be as costly as it seems.

Case History

The Hughes Helicopters Division of Summa Corporation does most of its selling at two trade shows–the military-oriented Association of the United States and the commercially oriented Helicopter Association of America. Not surprisingly, the company puts a great deal of emphasis on the presentations it develops for its exhibit area.

"The problem this organization faces," says Carl Perry, executive vice president at Hughes, "is that we have just about 5 or 6 seconds at these shows to capture prospects' attention as they pass by our booth. We need a way to stop them and grab their attention without being obnoxious or showy."

Their solution was a 7-minute presentation explaining how Hughes helicopters are used throughout the world. The presentation was put on in a 19-foot-diameter theatre-in-the-round, built specifically for the exhibit area. The theatre seated 15 people.

During one 3-day trade show, between 100 and 150 people saw the presentation every hour.

Although the presentation was expensive to produce, the company is more than pleased with its effectiveness. According to a survey conducted by *Flying Magazine*, about 25 percent of the last 100 purchasers of the Hughes 500D helicopter said their decision was influenced by the Hughes exhibit presentation.

Conference Room Meetings

Purpose

Most presentations of this type are meant to convey information. That information may consist of details of a new employee-benefit program, an outline of stages in a new project, the details of a department budget, an analysis of a market research study–in short, any and all information needed to keep an organization informed.

Audience

As the category description suggests, the size of an audience is usually limited to the number of people who can comfortably fit into a conference room or large office. Most conference room meetings are addressed to employees, although just about any group of people with a need for information is a potential audience. A purchasing agent may call in a group of vendors to explain new purchasing policies and procedures. A city official may invite community leaders to a presentation focusing on a new urban development plan. A school principal may outline new classroom programs to members of a school board.

As these few examples suggest, audience members for a conference room meeting may bring a variety of motivations to a presentation. Some may come to learn, others to support, still others to criticize, some just because they feel they're expected to attend. In some ways, this confusion of motivations makes it difficult for a presenter to tailor a message: there's no clear target to shoot at. If this is the case in a presentation you're preparing for, assume that, at the very least, your listeners will want to hear specific facts and figures. Any attempts to persuade or dissuade an audience should be subtly woven into this "informational" approach.

Production Considerations

For the most part, the factors discussed under the category "Sales–Person-to-Small-Group" also apply to this category. There are two exceptions, however. The first concerns equipment. Earlier we wrote that one of the most practical units for person to small group sales meetings was a desktop viewer. These units make travel and setup considerably easier for the sales rep. With general conference room meetings, however, the portability and convenience of equipment is not as critical. This type of meeting usually takes place within a presenter's organization, where equipment can be moved easily and set up well ahead of the presentation date. So it's the size of the room, not the portability of the equipment, that becomes the determining factor in equipment selection.

The second exception involves the length of a presentation. A sales rep is usually working under pressure. He or she must tell a story and ask for an order within a relatively short period of time. For that reason, sales presentations are kept brief. Presentations for a general meeting, on the other hand, usually have more time allotted to them. While there's still the need to keep the presentation as tight as possible, there's also the need to be certain that audience members fully understand the material being presented. If that takes 5 minutes, then the presentation should run 5 minutes. But if it takes 10 minutes, 20 minutes, or 30 minutes, the presenter must be prepared to devote that length of time to the presentation.

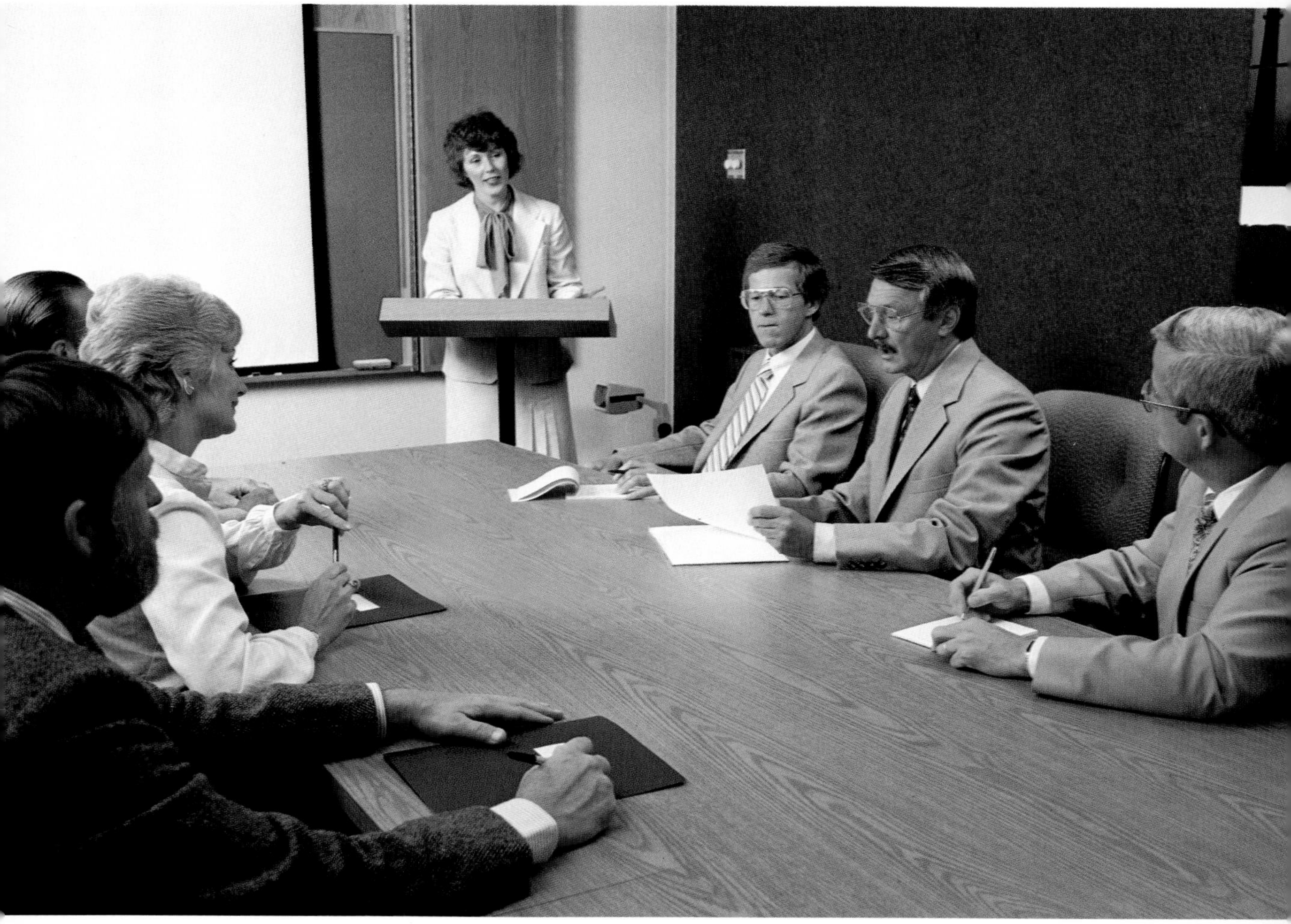

In a conference room presentation, audience members may reflect a wide variety of motivations.

Preparation

Presentation content determines the type of preparation undertaken. Some material, such as an explanation of a new company profit sharing plan, demands that a full script be written and a comprehensive storyboard be prepared. Information of this importance cannot be left to an improvised presentation.

Other material may require only an outline and slides made from existing charts or graphs. A presentation of a production schedule for an annual report, for example, wouldn't require a script and storyboard. Slides of an existing planning board, supplemented by artwork or photographs illustrating various production activities, could provide acceptable visual material. The presenter can talk from notes, or rely on memory for the basic information, using the visuals as cues for discussion of topics.

Analysis

The advantages and disadvantages of this type of presentation are similar to those presented under person-to-small-group sales meetings. One further point should be added, however, and that concerns the advantage of an

audiovisual presentation over single-dimension communication vehicles.

Pamphlets, booklets, and memos are effective forms of communication. So is the spoken word. But the impact of communication increases dramatically when information is addressed to both the eyes and ears. According to educational psychologists, that's because the more sensory inputs we can create in a learning situation, the greater the chances that people will recall the information presented. It's like using more than one hose to fill a bucket: the more hoses, the faster and more dramatic the filling process. The more channels to the brain, the faster and more thorough the information processing.

So why take the chance that some portion of your message will be missed or forgotten? Combine the impact of speech and visuals.

Case History

The State of California passed a law setting minimum standards for the protection of life and property against fire, explosion, and

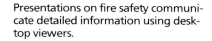

Presentations on fire safety communicate detailed information using desk-top viewers.

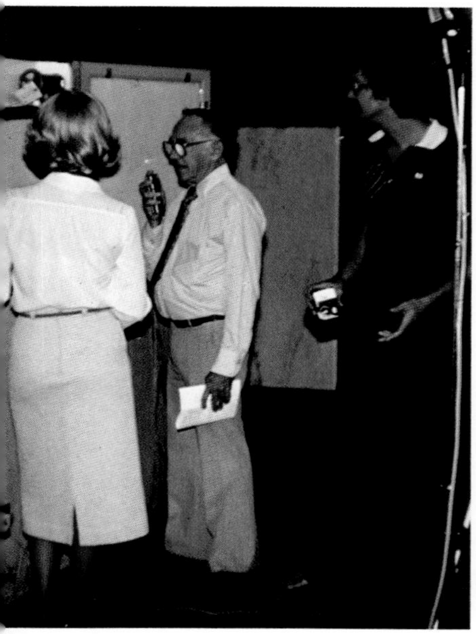

panic in high-rise buildings. For managers of these buildings, that law presented a communications problem. How would they present information on emergency procedures and evacuation routes to the hundreds, in some cases thousands, of people who worked or lived in these buildings?

The solution came in the form of a series of slide-tape presentations developed by Skyline Ventures, Inc., which sells the materials. The Los Angeles-based production company develops a specific presentation for each of its customers, with both narration and visuals reflecting the special problems and considerations affecting workers within a building. For some buildings, the script and visuals are actually refined to reflect specific conditions on a floor-by-floor basis.

The actual presentations, which are kept under 18 minutes, become the responsibility of the building manager. This individual makes the presentation using a desk-top viewer. The presentations are usually made to small groups, who are asked to attend the meeting during a coffee break. After the presentation is made, each member of the audience also receives a pamphlet reviewing the highlights of the presentation and duplicating the floor plan for his or her particular area.

The presentation format has been extremely effective and has been endorsed by fire chiefs from cities throughout California.

Multi-image

Purpose

A multi-image presentation isn't a true presentation type; rather, it's a sophisticated version of a number of the presentation types already discussed. Multi-image presentations are used extensively at general sales meetings, conferences, exhibits, annual meetings, and other gatherings where the size–or the importance–of the audiences justify the higher-than-average costs associated with multi-image production. The reason presenters decide to use multi-image techniques in creating specific presentations is to gain maximum impact. By using multiple images in a presentation controlled by sophisticated programming equipment, a presenter can add memorable emphasis to a message.

Audience

Depends on the specific type of presentation. See previous descriptions.

Production Considerations

1. Setting. To produce maximum impact, multi-image presentations require large presentation areas–auditoriums, convention halls, hotel ballrooms, specially built theatres. Because of the amount of equipment that's usually involved, these shows also require room for an extensive projection area. Adequate electrical power supplies are also a must.

2. Seating. Seating for multi-image presentations is usually arranged in a theatre-style pattern. It's especially important that the seating arrangement be carefully planned for multi-image presentations, because projectors are often set up at widely separated locations within the projection area, with their projection beams crossing on their way to the screen. This sort of setup can result in marginal seating areas along outer edges of the seating pattern. See page 107 for instructions on creating an effective viewing area.

3. Equipment. A multi-image presentation requires more equipment than any other type of audiovisual presentation. Numerous slide projectors are required. (Most multi-image presentations are produced for use with from three to nine projectors, although presentations using 20 or more projectors are not uncommon.) Each bank of slide projectors also requires a dissolve control. In some multi-image presentations, motion picture projectors also are used. These units, in turn, often require units that operate the projectors in precise synchronization with an audio-tape deck. Controlling all this equipment is a programmer. Most multi-image presentations also require a top-quality reel-to-reel tape playback unit, along with equally dependable amplification equipment and speakers.

4. Media. Most multi-image presentations use 2-by-2-inch slides as their basic medium. If film segments are to be integrated into the production, 16 mm motion picture film is used.

5. Length. The length of a multi-image presentation is determined by the purpose of the overall presentation. Some multi-image presentations, such as those used at exhibits, may not run much longer than 5 minutes. Others, such as those used at general sales meetings, usually run 30 minutes or more. Presentations of this length, however, require sophisticated production planning.

Multi-image presentations are an effective way to create a memorable impact.

6. Assistants. Absolutely. It would be next to impossible for a single presenter to put on a multi-image presentation involving more than two or three projectors. There's too much equipment involved and too many details for a single individual to attend to. The number of assistants required, of course, will depend on the sophistication of the presentation. In planning, however, remember that it's better to err by taking one too many assistants than by taking one too few.

Preparation

Preparations for a multi-image presentation are extensive. In fact, the initial planning that goes into preparing for a multi-image presentation may exceed all the work that goes into developing a full desk-top, point-of-purchase presentation. That being the case, this entry–in fact, this book–can't begin to describe the preparations that must be undertaken. If you're seriously considering producing a multi-image presentation, you would be well advised to study a book that covers the subject in depth. One such book, published by Eastman Kodak

Company, is *Images, Images, Images–The Book of Programmed Multi-Image Production*. It can be purchased at most audiovisual dealerships that sell Kodak products.

Analysis

1. Advantages. As stated earlier, the biggest advantage of a multi-image presentation is the impact it creates. If you've never seen a multi-image presentation, it may be hard for you to appreciate the validity of that claim. If you have, you know that multi-image presentations are to visual communication what the original *Life* magazine was to the field of photojournalism–another dimension, an extension of the definition of what's possible.

2. Disadvantages. It almost goes without saying. When you consider the hours that go into planning and producing a multi-image presentation, and when you consider the amount of equipment that must be assembled (and sometimes shipped), you know without even reaching for your calculator that you're talking about a sizable budget.

You're also talking about a longer-than-average production schedule. It's not unusual for a multi-image presentation to be in production for several months. Photography alone, which may result from 5,000 to 20,000 slides for a major production, can take months. Obviously then, a multi-image presentation can't be put together in a couple of days. Considerable time and money are involved, which is why most organizations save this type of presentation for occasions when the expenditures are almost certain to yield sufficient dividends.

Case History

The Pacific Telephone Company has found multi-image presentations to be an effective way to sell its services to business clients. In the past, because of facility limitations, Pacific Telephone sales reps used single-projector presentations to sell products and proposals. The company, however, recognized the potential of audiovisual selling, so it built a series of communications centers and equipped them with multi-image production and presentation equipment. Since then sales reps have been making multi-image presentations on the average of twice a month.

Each sales rep making a presentation writes a rough draft of a script, focusing on the specific requirements of a particular prospect. This script then goes to a production group, which polishes it and plans appropriate photography. Some slides are shot at the prospect's offices. Others come from the company's 9,000-slide library. Still others are created using art and graphs. The final step in the production process is programming.

The presentation itself, which is narrated by the sales rep, is given at a special meeting room equipped with three screens, 15 slide projectors, a variety of dissolve units, and a programmer.

The results of these custom-developed multi-image presentations have convinced company producers that their efforts are worth the time and money invested. They report that one of every three presentations results in an immediate sale.

Television Appearance

A television appearance is unlike any other presentation mentioned in this section.

For one thing, it's the only presentation in which the presenter doesn't see his or her audience. They're at home sitting in front of their television sets. That means there's no way for the presenter to know if his or her message is getting across.

A television appearance is also the only type of presentation in which the presenter doesn't have complete control of the situation. Control lies in the hands of the interviewer or program host. This person's intelligence, skill, and experience has as much–if not more–to do with the success of the presentation as the efforts of the presenter.

Finally, a television appearance is the only type of presentation in which there are few production considerations to worry about. Setting, seating, equipment, length–all these factors are the responsibilities of the television station and the producer of the show on which the presenter will appear. The presenter only need be concerned about content.

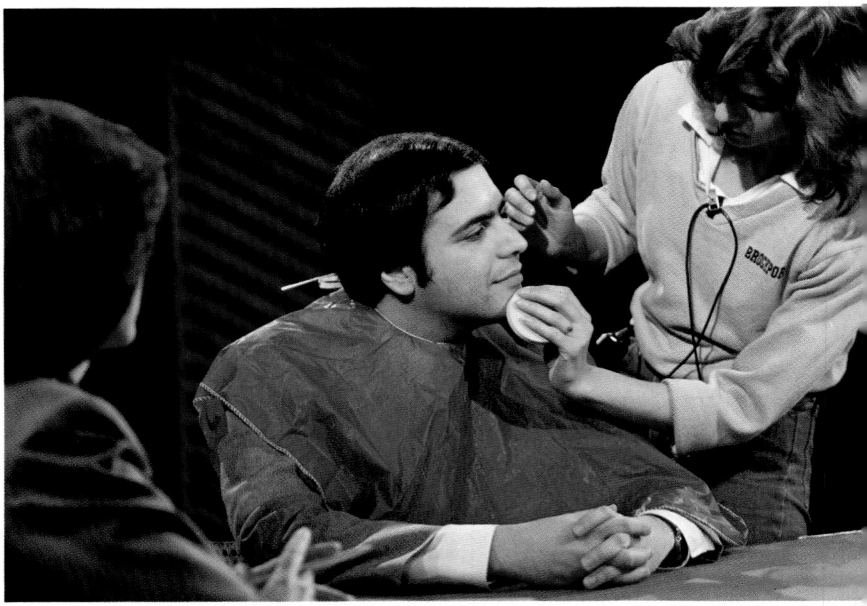

A television appearance requires a presenter to be a good conversationalist. But solid preparation also helps.

Of course, in one sense, a television appearance isn't even a presentation. It is–or should be– a conversation between an interviewer and his or her guest. The unseen audience members in front of their television sets are little more than welcome eavesdroppers.

But they are, after all, a very special group of eavesdroppers. It's this group that the presenter wants to reach, even though he or she will be talking to a program host.

What's the best way to reach these people? Experienced television producers offer the following suggestions:

• If you want to be invited to appear on a television program–whether a local news broadcast, a public service program, or a talk show–you have to think in terms of the needs of the station. And stations want features and guests that will attract viewers. That means that you must interest a station in what you have to say. You have to demonstrate the importance and newsworthiness of your topic. These people have to be convinced that what you have to say will appeal to a broad segment of their viewing community. If they're not convinced, you stand little chance of appearing on one of their programs.

In many cases, you'll also have to demonstrate the visual appeal of your subject matter. Television is a visual medium, and any visual material that allows a producer to eliminate "talking heads" adds to the appeal of your subject. (If you're not asked about visuals, it's still not a bad idea to show the producer the type of visuals you can provide. All other factors being equal, a guest with good visual support will probably get the nod over one without interesting visual material.)

• If you are invited to appear on a program, find out specifically what the interviewer wants to cover. Is he or she interested in all aspects of your subject? Or will time constraints force the interviewer to concentrate on one particular aspect? If the interviewer must narrow your topic, offer suggestions for areas that might prove most fruitful.

Also find out what type of visuals the producer wants. The easiest types of visuals to supply are 35 mm slides, shot in a horizontal format, or 16 mm motion picture segments. But make sure the slides or film segments are created with the television image area in mind. Otherwise you might lose part of your visual because it's too large for the television screen. Almost every station has the equipment needed to put slides and 16 mm film on the air. That may not be the case, however, if you supply super 8 film. Also, if a producer wants to use your slides or film, be sure to get them to the station a day or so ahead of your appearance. The producer will need time to review the materials and to pick out the sequences he or she would like to use. Time is also needed to load them into the film chain. Obviously, this work can't be performed at the last minute.

• Find out how much time will be devoted to you and your subject. If the producer is willing to devote considerable time–say more than 10 minutes–you won't have to worry much about the phrasing of your answers. But if you'll appear for only 3 to 5 minutes, give some thought to ways you can be brief. You might even try rehearsing your answers, with a colleague acting as the interviewer. Time your responses, try to keep your answers under a minute. In no case should you allow your answers to run beyond 2 minutes. On television, that's a long time—long enough to allow a viewer to lose interest and change stations.

• Memorize key facts, figures, and ideas, but don't overrehearse. You want your answers to sound like conversation, not a tape-recorded message. It's better to say that your organization is "almost twice as large as it was 3 years ago" than to say "membership has increased 92 percent over the last 36 months." The former sounds like conversation; the latter, like someone reading an annual report.

• When the interview begins, try to act as natural as possible. (More than likely you'll be nervous, but an experienced interviewer will try to make you feel at ease.) Speak as you would to an old friend. That means don't use jargon, legalese or the gobbledygook of the bureaucrat. Short, simple sentences are the best. And where possible, brighten your answers with an example or anecdote.

And since television is a visual medium, try to look alive. Use gestures and facial expressions, laugh if appropriate, do anything that makes you look like an enthusiastic, committed person.

And if you make a mistake—fine. Don't worry about it. Don't be afraid of it. Everyone makes mistakes or forgets a fact. Just admit it. Say you don't know. Viewers will find you more human and more believable.

• Don't use notes. It may be tempting to pull a note card out of your pocket or purse to help you through an answer. But avoid the temptation. Before 20 seconds has passed, the note card will become a crutch, and you'll be using it to prop yourself up through the rest of the interview. As mentioned above, it's better to say you don't know or you aren't sure than to read a prepared answer from a card.

• Finally, don't be afraid to use your appearance for your own benefit. You're not a witness whose answers must be confined to limits set by the question. If you think your host has missed the point with a question, say so. Then restate the question as you see proper and answer it the way you want to. All this, of course, is to be done tactfully and respectfully. You're not out to embarrass your host or to wrest control of the program from him or her. But you do have the right to steer the conversation to what you consider to be more fruitful areas, just as you would if you were sitting in a friend's living room. Your host probably won't mind. An animated, enthusiastic guest makes for good television.

3 Selecting Media and Equipment

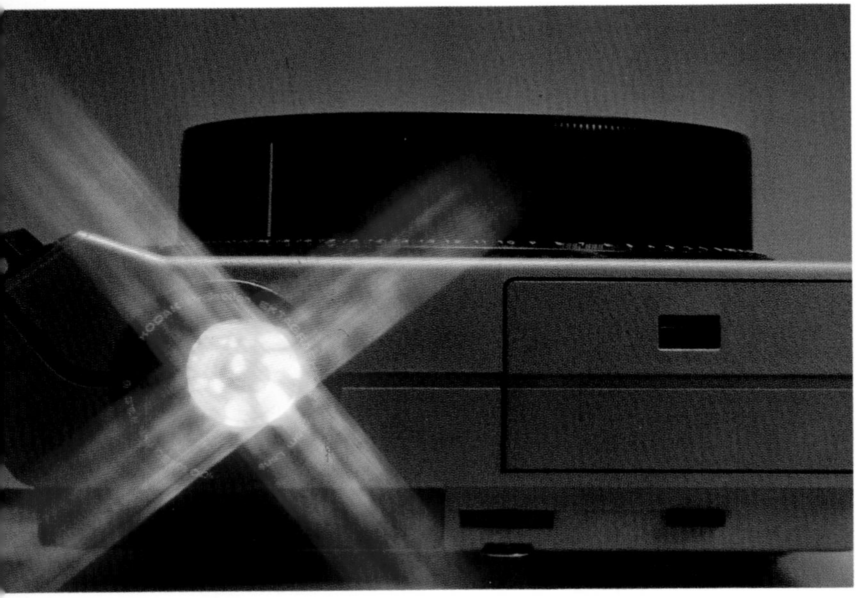

How will you present your visual materials?

Will you use slides? Film? Filmstrips? Overhead projection? Videotape?

Will you project your visuals with a single projector? Two projectors? A dozen or more projectors? A self-contained desk-top viewer?

Will you control projection remotely? Will an assistant help you? Or will the presentation be controlled automatically by dissolve units linked to a multi-image programmer?

Obviously, as you begin to prepare for a presentation, you have a lot of options open to you. That's why many people enjoy this aspect of preparation. They're like kids with a toy catalogue in the weeks before Christmas. There's so much to choose from, it's hard to know where to start.

That's why it's important to put your presentation—and your preparations—into perspective. And to do that, you have to take the time to examine two factors. First, you have to study the type of presentation you're going to give. Each type of presentation is characterized by certain requirements and limitations. A desk-top presentation, for example, requires portable, easy-to-use equipment, and that fact alone limits what you'll be able to do visually. So as you consider the type of presentation you're planning for, ask yourself, what is it *possible* to do?

Second, you have to examine the resources available to you—the money, time, and talent you'll have to produce your materials. Naturally, the more you have of each resource, the more you should be able to do. But if you're on your own with a small budget and a tight deadline, you have to scale down your creative aspirations. So here again, as you weigh your resources, ask yourself, what is it *possible* to do?

Once you know what's possible, you have the perspective you need to select your media and equipment.

Before we look at media and equipment, however, let's examine each of the above considerations a little more closely.

Type of Presentation

The various types of presentations examined in the previous chapter can be divided into two broad categories. First there's the "really big show"—a platform presentation, a workshop or lecture, a multi-image presentation, or an exhibit. This type of presentation involves larger audiences that are usually seated over a wide area. Because of this, you have to think big when you consider media and equipment. You need images, projection equipment, and screens scaled to the size of your site and your audience. You also need audio equipment that can fill the presentation site with rich, true-to-life sound. So when you're putting on a "really big show," you must prepare to reach the last person in the last row at the presentation site.

The second type of presentation is the "person-to-person" performance—a tabletop presentation or meeting involving a comparative handful of people. These presentations are more intimate, so there should be more emphasis on the presenter and not on equipment. That means you must scale down your equipment requirements to the dimensions and atmosphere of the immediate presentation area—whether it's a sales counter or a conference room.

A television appearance is a special type of presentation, and for the most part you don't have to worry about equipment as you prepare. Most stations have the equipment to project slides, 16 mm motion picture film, and ¾-inch or larger videotape. But that's not always true of super 8 film, so if some of your visual material is contained on super 8, check with the station. If they have a film chain that allows them to go directly onto the air with super 8, you'll have no problems. If their equipment requires them to make a film-to-tape transfer first, you'll have to get your footage to the station ahead of your scheduled appearance. If they have no way of using super 8 film, you'll have to find or prepare other materials.

The Budget

There's no way around it–it costs money to produce a presentation. You need money for supplies: film, slide mounts, audiotape. Then there are film processing costs. And you have to add in all the labor costs: your own hours plus the charges made by writer, photographer, audiotape editor, assistants, and others whose skills you may need. You may also have costs for equipment, whether they're purchase prices or rental fees. And if your presentation is going on the road, you'll have shipping costs for your equipment and travel expenses for you and any assistants. Finally, incidental costs, such as for promoting your presentation, also have to be included in your budget. As you can see, figuring your presentations budget is going to require a calculator and a lot of patience.

The figure on the bottom line depends, of course, on the length and sophistication of your presentation. A presentation produced from available slides and made with a single projector or a desktop projector doesn't have to be expensive. Of course, if you have to buy the equipment and if your hours have to be charged to the project, even this simple presentation can cost from $500 to $1,000. And if you're thinking about a major multi-image presentation, then you better start thinking about a major budget, too. Some of the more elaborate multi-image presentations produced in recent years reportedly have had budgets reaching into six figures.

Budgeting, of course, is a process that can be approached in two ways. You can start with a specified sum of money, then see what sort of presentation can be produced for that sum. Or you can start with an idea, then determine what it's going to cost to turn that idea into a reality. Either way, you have to place dollar amounts next to each cost category. If you have some experience in audiovisual production, this process won't be too difficult. But if you don't have experience, you have some learning to do. Start with different categories of costs you have to budget for. Then find an expert who can help you fill in the blanks. Maybe there's a photographer or audio-

Before shooting slides for a presentation, calculate the costs involved in all phases of production.

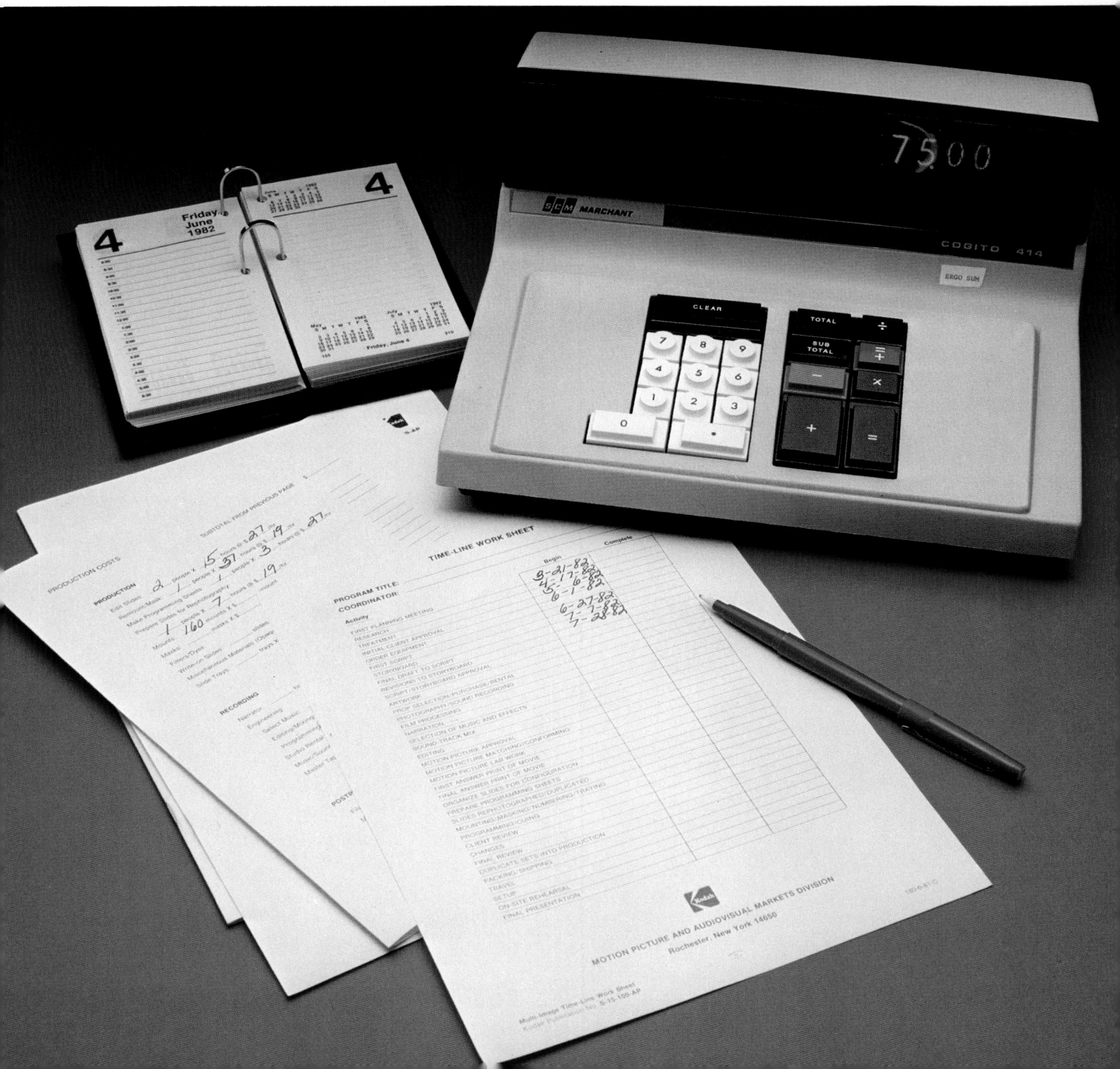

visual specialist in your organization who can advise you. If there isn't, try your local audiovisual dealer. He or she may be able to help you develop some general costs, especially for film, processing, materials, and equipment. The labor costs you'll have to develop yourself. Airlines and shipping companies can help you with transportation costs.

As you work on your budget, keep one thought in mind: It's not the amount of money you have that determines the success of your production, it's what you do with that money. So be realistic; don't expect a flow of purchase orders to be the answer to your problem.

Time

In audiovisual production, as in life, money isn't everything. You may have enough money in your budget to produce a 24-projector multi-image presentation, but if you don't have the time on your calendar to devote to the project, you better approach your preparations by considering what time will allow.

During planning, allow sufficient time and money for preparing sound tracks and for editing and sequencing slides.

In planning for a presentation, you have to allow time for overall production planning, scriptwriting, photography and processing, production (preparing visuals and, if necessary, audio tracks), rehearsals and, if your presentation is being made out of town, shipping.

Here again, your ability to develop a schedule for these activities will depend on your experience. If you've produced a number of audiovisual presentations, you won't have much trouble. If you don't have the experience, look for someone within your organization to help you. If the in-house expertise isn't available, try asking your local audiovisual dealer for advice. As you gather your time estimates, use the planning sheet on page 83 to prepare your schedule.

One of the best ways to develop this schedule is to work backward. Start with the scheduled date of your presentation. Then, working backwards on a calendar, count off the number of days needed for shipping (if that's necessary). You now have the latest date on which you can ship your equipment with a reasonable hope of on-time delivery. Once you've marked this date, count back until you've allowed for the number of days needed for rehearsals. You now have the date on which all production activities must be completed. Continue working this way until you've allotted time and marked deadlines for all of your production activities.

You're in good shape if the schedule falls comfortably between the current date and the date of the presentation. Your schedule contains what planners call "slack"—a time cushion that can absorb a missed deadline or two. But if you're smack up against the starting date—or worse yet, if your schedule says you should have started work already—you're going to have some rescheduling to do.

One way to make up time—the most expensive way—is to buy it. You can use some of your budget to hire extra people. If your schedule indicates that your show can be produced by one person working 30 days, you may be able to complete it in about half that time using two or more people. The catch, of course, is that the project is going to cost you more than twice as much.

Another way to save a schedule is to reduce your expectations. Reexamine your presentation, looking for elements you can eliminate or simplify. Maybe you don't need motion picture film segments. Maybe you don't need multi-image. Maybe you can cut your presentation from 30 minutes to 20 minutes or less. Revisions such as these will save you time.

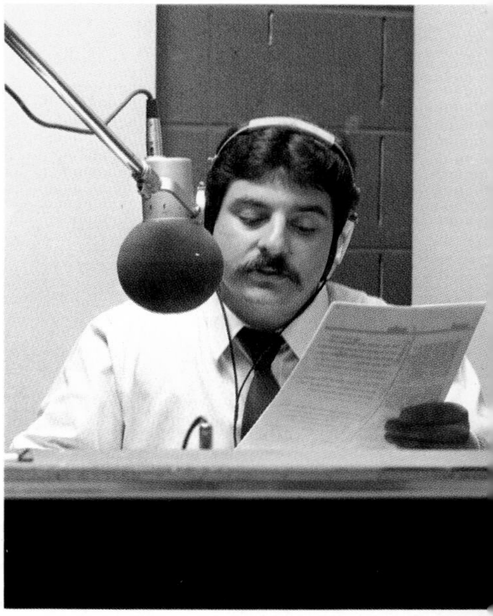

Talent

In some cases, this may be the most limiting factor in your production considerations. If you must work alone, then your talents determine the sophistication of your presentation. What does this mean in terms of selecting media and equipment? Well, if you're working on your first presentation, keep it simple: Plan to use slides, working with one or two projectors. Use a tabletop unit if you're presenting to a small group. But don't try to set the world on fire with your first presentation; you may be the one who winds up getting burned.

If, on the other hand, you're experienced in audiovisual production, working alone doesn't have to mean a simple presentation. You can select whatever media and equipment you're familiar with. Just be practical: Evaluate your talent and experience in terms of the time available.

If you're planning to work with specialists in slide, film, or audio production, you face a different sort of talent consideration. You must make certain that the talent's available when you need it. Don't go out and round up a dozen projectors for a multi-image presentation on the assumption you'll find a producer. You may not. In fact, the more sophisticated the production techniques involved, the more difficult it is to find people with the requisite talent. Finding a producer to put together a three-projector presentation may be easy. Finding one with the

experience to produce a major multi-image presentation complete with film segments, laser lights, and holographic displays may keep you on the phone for days. And when you finally find the right person, you might also find that his or her time is scheduled for the next 9 months. So don't select your equipment or media first; select your talent.

Media

Now you have some perspective. You've set presentation goals. You know what's required for different types of presentations. And you know how much time, talent, and money you have for production. With these considerations in mind, you can begin to choose your media and equipment.

Slides. The 2-by-2-inch slide (the dimensions refer to the outer measurements of the slide mount) is by far the most popular visual medium used in presentations. The reasons presenters give for choosing slides are these:

• Slides are a less costly medium. Film and processing costs are less for slides than for filmstrips or motion picture production. In fact, the only medium that's less costly than slides is the acetate transparency used for overhead projectors. The acetate transparency, however, has a much more restricted use. For all-around versatility, slides are often the more practical production choice.

• Slides are easy to shoot and process. The cameras are light and easy to use, and the techniques involved are less complicated. And processing services are available through your local audiovisual dealer, a camera shop, or even a corner drugstore.

• Slides are easier to work with. Editing film or videotape is a process that requires special equipment and training. That's not so with slides. All you need to edit slides is an illuminator. You can select the shots you want, arrange and rearrange them, load them into a slide tray, and project them, and if you aren't satisfied with the sequence, you can repeat the process again. While that's also possible, to some extent, with motion picture film, the process is more complicated and time-consuming. It's even more complicated with videotape.

• Slides are easier to change at a later date. You can change a sequence in a slide presentation by simply removing and replacing slides. This makes it easy to keep your presentation up to date. It also allows you to adapt your presentation to your audience. If, for example, you're making a presentation in different areas of the country, you can plan an easily modified sequence containing slides of locally prominent landmarks and institutions. New slides can be inserted into the sequence for each area visited. Some presenters adapt the length of their presentations this way. They produce a full version of their presentation, then simply remove certain sections when they have to shorten their performances.

If you're planning to use slides, you can choose from three common image sizes. The *135 slide*—most people call it a 35 mm slide—is the most popular slide format for presentations. It offers the best overall balance of cost, image size, emulsion variety, and film speed.

Some presenters prefer to use *super-slides*, especially if their presentations must use extremely large projected images or if they're making their presentations in areas with high ambient light.

You can also use the *126* format slide. This format was developed for use in cameras such as the Kodak Instamatic® Camera. Its smaller image area means you'll have to work with shorter projection distances if you want to maintain picture quality. This format is used most often in presentations produced for and by schools.

The chart on page 175 gives image area dimensions and projection distances for each of the slide formats.

Filmstrips. This is a hybrid medium. Filmstrip images, like motion picture images, are contained on a continuous length of film, which is driven through a projector by a sprocket advance mechanism. But the images are shown individually, like slides.

The advantages of this medium are in its packaging. An 80-image filmstrip can be shipped or stored in a container not much larger than a D-cell battery. An 80-slot slide tray, by contrast, is far larger and heavier.

Filmstrips are also somewhat easier to use. A presenter doesn't have to worry about images being in the right order. The order is set in the processing lab. So out-of-sequence mix-ups or upside-down images caused by improper loading are eliminated. This benefit is especially important when the presentation will be put on by people other than the producer.

But many presenters consider these advantages to be of minor importance when compared with the disadvantages of using filmstrips. To begin with, there's an extra production step involved. Once slides are selected for a presentation, they have to be sent to a lab and copied to produce the filmstrip. This involves not only additional time, but also additional cost. What's more, once a filmstrip is completed, it can't be changed without duplicating the process. Again, time and money are involved. Finally, filmstrips just aren't suited for more sophisticated presentations using multi-image production techniques.

Filmstrips are available in four image sizes. The largest and most popular is 35 mm. Also available are 16 mm, 8 mm, and super 8 formats. The latter is often used in portable desk-top filmstrip projectors.

Overhead transparencies. For ease of production, it's hard to beat acetate transparencies for overhead projection. You can prepare visual material in minutes using a grease pencil or a marking pen to create words, charts, or art directly on an acetate sheet. (In fact, you can create—or add to—a transparency during the course of a presentation.)

If you want a "cleaner" look for your transparencies, you can create them using letter templates or dry transfer type. You can also create transparencies with a typewriter, but to assure adequate legibility, you must use a primary-size typeface. These methods take slightly longer than freehand techniques, but not much. In most cases, this additional time is worth taking. The resulting visuals will not only be more legible, they'll also be more emphatic, if for no other reason than they suggest greater preparation.

Finally, transparencies can be prepared using a variety of copying techniques. Some office copying machines will make adequate transparencies in very short time, although they're usually best when used only with type or line art. If high-quality transparencies are important to your presentation, photographic reproduction is the most effective method. (Photographic reproduction is also the only method that allows you to change the size of the original material.) This method is more costly and takes more time than other approaches, but it's also the only method that can produce the visual impact created by slides.

Overhead transparencies are also easy to use. During a presentaton, a transparency is placed on an overhead projector's "stage"–an illuminated glass surface. (The most commonly used transparency consists of an 8-by-10-inch acetate sheet, mounted in a plastic or paperboard frame. The dimensions of the transparency fall within the aperture area of most "stages.")

The transparency stays on the "stage" while the presenter discusses the material it contains. If it is a single-subject transparency, the presenter must change transparencies when moving to the next subject. If the transparency consists of overlays, or if it uses masks for progressive disclosures or selective disclosures, the base transparency stays in place while the new material is "added" to the display.

This necessity to remove transparencies from the "stage" (and thus from the screen) ranks as the major drawback of overhead projection. Out of consideration for an audience, a presenter should turn off the projector's lamp during the changeover. If it is left on, it will produce an intense glare that might prove discomforting or annoying to an audience. By turning the lamp out, the presenter also eliminates a potential cause of distraction–the moving image that would be projected while the next transparency is positioned.

A further drawback is the amount of space required to store transparencies. Unlike slides, which can be stored in small cartons kept in a desk drawer, transparencies should be stored in folders that are placed upright in a file cabinet. This is the only way to keep them clean, wrinkle-free and dust-free.

Motion pictures. In nine out of ten presentations, slides are the ideal medium for visual information. In that tenth presentation, however, motion is essential. An action must be shown–an assembly procedure or a new medical technique has to be demonstrated, or the results of a research test are to be explained using high-speed film sequences. In cases like these, only motion pictures will suffice.

If your planned presentation absolutely needs motion, consider using one of the following formats:

The most common format is 16 mm film. The reasons:

• Production equipment is readily available. If your organization doesn't own a 16 mm camera or 16 mm editing equipment, it can rent these units from a motion picture rental company.

• Production quality is better than that for super 8. A frame of 16 mm film offers an image area considerably larger than that of super 8, so there's more surface on which to record the details of a scene. This usually means better definition, crisper color, and less grain in the final print. In addition, while there are many good super 8 cameras on the market, the optics and operation of 16 mm cameras are generally more sophisticated. Also, unlike super 8, there are 16 mm film stocks and film systems for origination, intermediates, and duplication.

When motion is required in visual sequences, the most commonly used medium is 16 mm motion picture film.

• The projected image is more suitable for large audiences. This is also a matter of image size. The larger the image area through which light can travel, the longer the distance an image can be projected. This factor is of considerable importance if you're planning to use motion picture sequences along with slides. That means if you're projecting slide and film images of about the same size, you'll want the image brightness on the screen to be as uniform as possible.

Super 8 film is often the choice of presenters who must show action in presentations to small groups, especially if the presentation is one that will be given at a number of locations. Because of its compact size, super 8 film can be used with portable, self-contained projectors that can be placed on top of a table. This scaling down of equipment not only reduces the number of pieces of equipment needed, it also prevents the film and equipment from dominating a performance.

Audiotape. If segments of your presentation are to be "canned"—what broadcasters now call "prerecorded"— you have to select the type of audiotape you're going to work with. Most producers work with two types of audiotape: ¼-inch tape in reel-to-reel form, or audiotape cassettes.

The ¼-inch tape is used almost exclusively during initial recording sessions, whether in a studio or on location. This choice is the result of two factors. First, recording equipment for ¼-inch tape is generally superior to cassette recorders. They offer faster recording speeds (the faster the recording speed, the better the sound quality). And they can be used with a wider range of microphones, most of which are usually of better quality than those used with cassette recorders. Second, editing ¼-inch tape is far easier than editing the smaller cassette tape.

When it comes to the actual presentation, however, either format is acceptable. The choice usually depends on the type of presentation. Most producers choose ¼-inch tape for major, expensive productions. In these cases, they're looking for the slightly better sound quality given by ¼-inch playback equipment. On the other hand, a producer putting on a

one- or two-projector presentation to a small group generally chooses an audiotape cassette. He or she prefers the convenience of the cassette, plus the added benefit of small, lighter weight equipment. In addition, many cassette playback units can be used to control projection equipment.

Equipment

Slide projectors. Choosing a slide projector can be like choosing a car. Many different models are available, each with many different features. Eastman Kodak Company, for example, sells 15 models of its extremely popular Kodak Ektagraphic Slide Projector. Considering the wide range of equipment available, your best approach when you set out to choose a projector is to balance product features with your needs.

Here's a list of some basic features you should consider when you select slide projectors for your presentation. (If you'd like detailed,

Most professionals use ¼-inch audio tape for recording sound. For playback, either ¼-inch tape or audio cassettes are acceptable.

current information on Kodak's complete line of slide and motion picture projectors, see your local audiovisual dealer. Or write to Eastman Kodak Company, Motion Picture and Audiovisual Division, and ask for a copy of the most recent *KODAK Audiovisual Products Catalog*.)

• *Rugged construction.* Slide projectors used for presentations receive a lot of rough handling, especially if they're shipped for out-of-town performances. So look for a housing that's made of metal or heavy-duty plastic.

• *Long-life motor.* Consider how often you'll use your projector as you prepare and present your material. Multiply that by the number of presentations you'll give over the course of several years. That buildup of hours is the reason a heavy-duty motor is essential.

• *Slide versatility.* Slides are often mounted in a variety of ways: cardboard, glass, metal, or plastic. You need a projector that can handle all of these mounts without jamming.

• *Uniform image brightness.* The quality of your projected image will be influenced by image size, lamp output, lens speed, and the general quality of the lens optics. An audiovisual dealer can help you select the right combination of lamp output and lens features for your presentation.

• *A selection of lamp settings.* By allowing you to select between "high" and "low" lamp settings, a projector can extend the life of a lamp. Use the "low" setting when you're preparing your presentation and when you're giving it in a small room. Use the "high" setting for large-room presentations.

• *Remote control.* This is an absolute must, if you're working without an assistant. During a presentation, you should be standing near your screen, not your projectors. And the only way you can do this is if you have a remote-control unit that allows you to control the operation of the projector. Remote-control units are of two types: The more common–and simplest–unit consists of a handheld advance/reverse/focus control connected to a projector by a long cord. More sophisticated units offer a wider range of control functions, contained in either handheld or podium-mounted wireless transmitters.

• *Automatic focus.* This feature automatically focuses slides as they drop into the projector gate. It frees you to concentrate on your narration, not on the quality of the screen image. (Automatic focus should be used only with slides in similar mounts. If you'll be using slides with different type mounts, you'll need automatic focus override control.)

• *Convenient leveling apparatus.* Your presentation won't look professional if your projectors are elevated and leveled using books and ashtrays. Select a projector in which the elevating and leveling apparatus are easy to reach and use.

• *Zoom lens.* A zoom lens allows you to vary the size of your projected image without having to move your projectors. This is an especially important feature if you'll be making presentations in rooms of different sizes.

In addition to these features, you may find some of the following accessories important to your preparations or presentation:

Choose a slide projector that meets both current and future presentation requirements.

Dissolve controls give multi-projector presentations an uninterrupted visual flow.

• *Stack loader.* This allows you to project and edit up to forty 2-by-2-inch slides without loading them into a slide tray. It's a time-saver when working on major presentations.

• *Filmstrip adapter.* This unit enables you to project 35 mm single-frame filmstrips without having to change the condenser lens in your projector.

• *A sound synchronizer.* Permits you to use a stereo recorder with external speaker jacks to program and control your projector.

• *An automatic timer* allows automatic slide changing. The KODAK EC Automatic Timer, Model III, for example, is continuously variable from approximately 3 seconds to 22 seconds.

If your projectors are to be used for traveling presentations, you should also consider the purchase of protective carrying cases. These cases not only protect your projectors, they also give you room to carry a spare tray, an extra lens, a spare lamp, and extension cords.

Dissolve controls. If your presentation uses more than one slide projector, consider the use of a dissolve control. This unit allows you to blend images into each other, giving a presentation an uninterrupted visual flow. Many manufacturers sell dissolve controls, with each offering slightly different features. The simpler units link two projectors and offer a limited number of screen effects—usually either a "fast" dissolve or a "slow" dissolve. Next come slightly more sophisticated units that offer both dissolve and quick-change features with continuously variable dissolve rates, flashing, freeze-frame, and more. The most sophisticated dissolve controls, used with multi-image programmers, link three projectors and offer a wider variety of effects.

Self-contained slide-tape equipment. These units contain a slide projector, audiotape player, and screen, all in a compact, portable case. They're the ideal unit for salespeople and others who have to make a number of presentations every day, usually at different sites. They eliminate the need to worry about setup requirements or the placement of screen or

Self-contained slide/tape equipment offers considerable convenience during production and presentation.

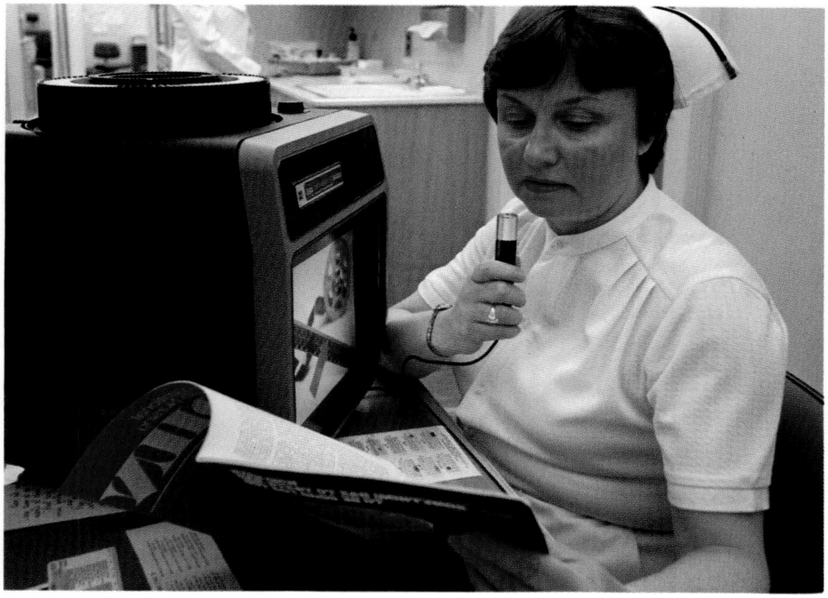

speakers. All the presenter has to do is plug in the power cord, and the unit's ready to go.

The KODAK EKTAGRAPHIC Audioviewer/Projector uses 80-slide or 140-slide trays. Some models of the Audioviewer/Projector can also be used to record an audiotape cassette. All models offer a playback feature. Two models of the unit also allow a presenter to program a presentation using audio tones to advance slides.

Filmstrip projectors. These units are also available in sizes and capabilities to meet the needs of any presenter. Some units are similar in size and features to self-contained slide projection equipment. Their rear-projection screens are suitable for presentations to small audiences. On the other end of the scale are units large enough to use in classrooms, workshops, and at other presentations made to moderately sized audiences. Most filmstrip projectors aren't suitable for projection in large meeting areas.

Overhead projectors. This equipment is used most often in classroom or workshop presentations and for meetings. In one sense, overhead projectors are more closely related to flipcharts than they are to slide presentations. Just as a presenter would flip the page of a chart to move on to new information, he or she removes a transparency from the projector's frosted glass aperture and inserts a new one. In fact, in many presentations, a presenter may use a marker to highlight or add information to a projected transparency. In some cases, the presenter may actually start with a blank transparency sheet and create the visual as the presentation develops.

Overhead projectors are of two types: The true overhead projector uses transparent acetate sheets for its visual images. An opaque projector uses pages from books or magazines, flat charts or graphics, typed or computer-printed data summaries, even handwritten notes or sketches for its visual images. This latter approach, of course, should be used only for the most informal type of presentation.

Motion picture projectors. Your choice here, of course, depends on what type of film you're using. And it's quite a choice you have. Dozens of manufacturers offer a variety of models for each film format. Selecting the one that best suits your needs can take considerable time and analysis.

As you narrow down your selection, remember there's one quality above all others that you want in a motion picture projector. And you should demand it whether you're choosing an attaché-case-size unit for super 8 desk-top projection or a large theatre-size projector for use with major podium presentations. That quality is dependability. You want a projector that won't tear your film or lose its film loops midway through your presentation. When that happens, all the effort that went into creating a smoothly flowing presentation is lost. Your continuity of ideas, mood, and rhythm is broken.

If you don't want this to happen to you, select a projector with a reputation for reliability.

But whatever projector you select, make sure it has at least the following features:

- optical and magnetic playback
- amplifier power great enough to allow your sound to reach all corners of the presentation site
- focusing sound optics to provide greatest clarity and fidelity in sound playback

If you think you'll be using your projector in many different presentation sites, also consider the ability to change projection lenses.

Multi-image programmers. Multi-image programmers and their related equipment allow presenters to pack their presentations with visual wallop. At the least sophisticated end of the scale, multi-image programmers can control from three to six projectors. At the other end of the scale, where programming technology is merging with computer technology, programmers are being built that can control more than 100 projectors, using more than 10,000 stored commands.

Of course, in order to understand—and appreciate—what this sort of equipment can do for a presentation, you have to be somewhat familiar with multi-image programming techniques. It isn't until you've programmed an animation sequence that you begin to appreciate the advantages of a built-in programming feedback loop.

This book isn't meant to be an introduction to multi-image programming or equipment. It's a highly specialized, rapidly changing field, one you shouldn't tackle until you've had some experience with more basic audiovisual presentations. If you have experience and are interested in learning more about multi-image production and presentation, we suggest you start with the book *Images,*

Often you can achieve spectacular results on a modest budget by renting equipment you can't afford to buy.

Images, Images–The Book of Programmed Multi-Image Production (S-12), published by Eastman Kodak Company. You also might consider attending a workshop devoted to multi-image presentation techniques. Kodak offers such workshops through its Marketing Education Center. Other workshops are offered by groups such as the Association for Multi-Image.

Buy or Rent

Equipment budgets aren't for the faint of heart. You could easily spend your entire presentation budget for a year and still not have all your basic equipment. Consider some of the costs: At the very least you're going to need a basic slide projector. If you also need a good, all-purpose screen, add even more to your budget. With those two purchases, you're equipped to give a very simple presentation. Thinking about a major presentation, something spectacular with loads of dazzling effects? You may need one of the more sophisticated multi-image programmers, complete with dissolve controls, a dozen or so projectors, a top-quality tape recorder, and other related equipment. Price: upwards of $30,000. That's a figure that might cause you to shudder, but don't forget that your purchase is a capital item and can be depreciated and amortized over several years.

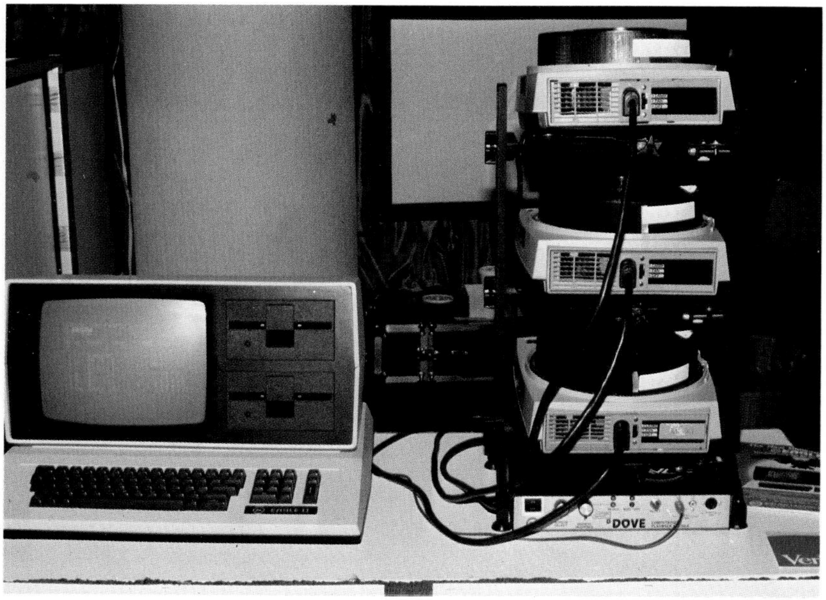

But to be realistic, you don't have to spend thousands of dollars to get the right equipment for your presentation. The best approach–at first–is to buy the basic equipment and rent whatever else you need. Although rental prices vary, equipment is usually about 10 percent of the purchase price on a one-day rental and there's usually a cost break for renting by the week.

What's basic? That, in a sense, depends on your aspirations. But at the very least, you should have the following:

- at least two 2-by-2-inch slide projectors with matched lenses
- one 16 mm motion picture projector
- a half dozen 80-slot slide trays
- a basic dissolve unit (for use with two-projector slide presentations)
- a slide illuminator/organizer
- carrying cases for your projectors
- a portable screen

This equipment enables you to produce and give a simple presentation. Once you have the above equipment, consider adding the following items:

- a cassette playback unit with slide synchronizing capability (for use with the dissolve unit)
- if you must shoot most of the photography yourself, also consider buying a 35 mm still camera.

If you'll be responsible for developing and giving a number of presentations throughout the course of a year, you also might consider buying a reel-to-reel tape recorder with editing capability and a professional-quality copy stand.

Beyond this point it gets harder and harder to justify the purchase of additional equipment, especially if major presentations aren't part of your job description. Additional money, if available, might be better spent buying several more slide projectors plus additional lenses and accessories to be used with your basic equipment.

Whenever you need more specialized equipment, you can usually rent it from an audiovisual dealer or an audiovisual rental company. Depending on their size, these companies usually rent such equipment as:

- 16 mm motion picture projectors
- 16 mm motion picture editing equipment
- 16 mm motion picture production equipment (cameras, tripods, sound recording equipment)
- theatre-size screens
- special projection lenses
- speakers and amplifiers for theatre sound systems

Of course, in many cases you may not have to rent equipment. You can hire the services of an audiovisual specialist and produce your presentation using his or her equipment. Film producers, for example, must have 16 mm production and editing equipment. Sound recording specialists will have all the equipment needed for recording and editing. And staging companies are a good source, too. So if you find yourself in need of specialized equipment, consider obtaining equipment and specialist together. Look in the Yellow Pages under "AV Equipment and Supplies."

Using Worksheet 2

This work sheet pulls together the information presented in the previo two chapters. The first–and easier–section of the work sheet requires you to determine the type of presen tation you plan to give. Next, you ha to establish the factors that will influ ence your planning for budget and schedule.

That's the second section of the wor sheet–putting figures and dates into your overall presentation plan. This section is going to be tough to complete. In fact, if you haven't had muc experience with presentation produ tion and planning, you may want to get an "old pro" to help you pull together your initial estimates. You should be able to get help from an audiovisual specialist in your organization, from an independent producer (but only if you intend to pay for this counseling or if you plan to give some of the production work to the producer), or from an audiovisu dealer in your area.

Plan alone or with an experienced assistant–it doesn't matter how you plan just as long as you do it. But don't skip these pages hoping to avoid the effort involved in thoroug planning. You can't.

If you don't plan for your presentatio now, you'll have to do it later. Unfortunately, people who wait to plan usually find themselves working the way out of a problem.

Worksheet 2 Selecting Media and Equipment

I. Type of presentation (from Chapter 2):

Purpose:
To

Size of audience: Setting: Seating:

Length: Assistants: No ☐ Yes ☐ How many?

II A. Budget:

People:		$
	Your time:	$
	Writer:	$
	Photographer:	$
	Sound Engineer:	$
	Programmer:	$
	Producer:	$
	Assistants:	$
	On-stage talent:	$
	Others:	$

		Needed (Y/N)	Purchase Price	Rental Fee
Equipment:	Slide projectors		$	$
	Dissolve control		$	$
	Self-contained viewer		$	$
	Filmstrip projector		$	$
	Overhead projector		$	$
	16 mm motion picture projector		$	$
	super 8 motion picture projector		$	$
	multi-image programmer		$	$
	screens		$	$

Supplies:	Slide film	$
	Acetate sheets	$
	Motion picture film	$
	Audiotape	$
	Film processing	$
	Slide mounts	$
Other:	Travel:	$
	Shipping:	$
	Promotion:	$
Total:		$

II B. Schedule:

Deadline: When will the presentation be given?

Working days available as of today:

How will this time be divided?

	deadline	# of days
Planning:		
Scriptwriting:		
Photography:		
Film Processing:		
Sound Recording:		
Sound Editing:		
Visual Editing:		
Production:*		

*The linking of audio and visual elements. With simple desk-top presentations, this step may require only hours; with large multi-image productions, this step may require days or weeks of programming.

Many producers include contingency funds in their budget estimates to cover changes, delays, and other unanticipated events. In some productions, this contingency fund may equal about 10 percent of the total production estimate.

4 Developing Script and Visuals

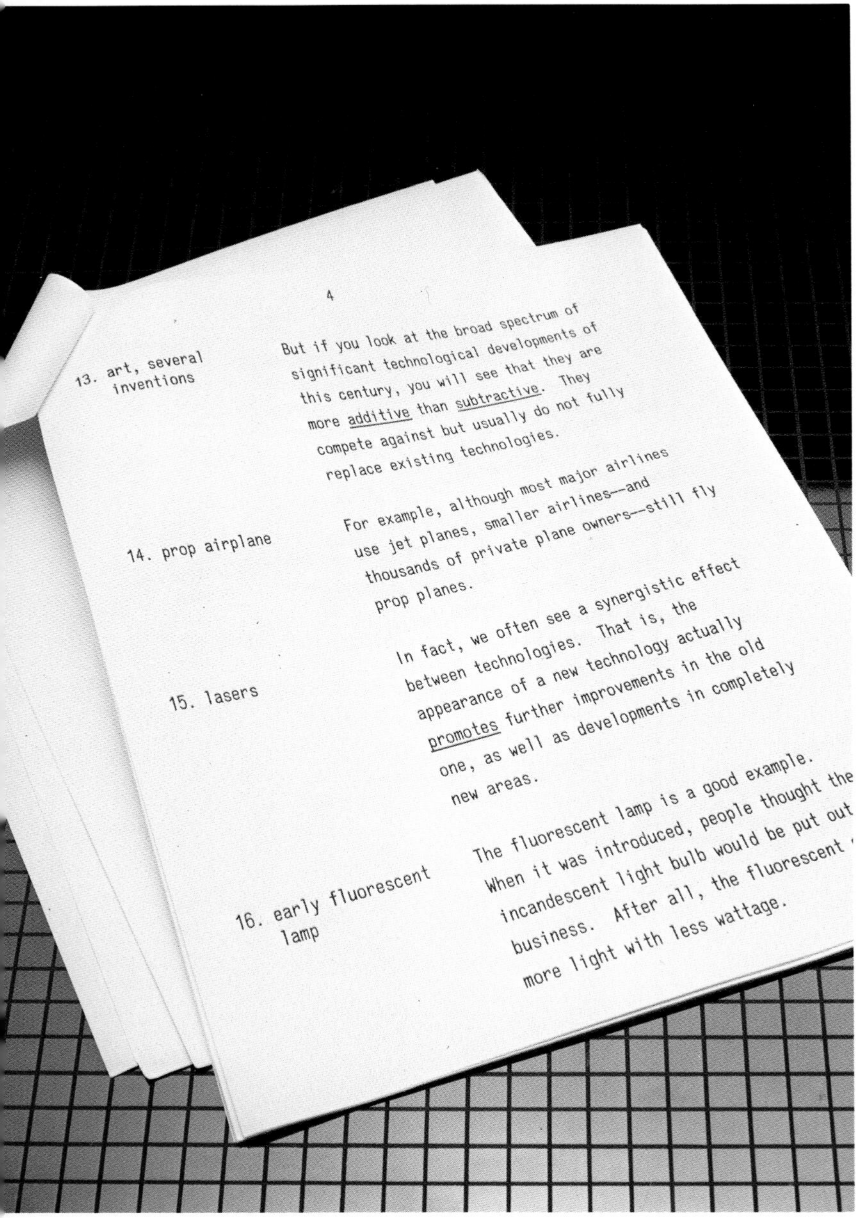

4
13. art, several inventions
But if you look at the broad spectrum of significant technological developments of this century, you will see that they are more additive than subtractive. They compete against but usually do not fully replace existing technologies.
14. prop airplane
For example, although most major airlines use jet planes, smaller airlines--and thousands of private plane owners--still fly prop planes.
15. lasers
In fact, we often see a synergistic effect between technologies. That is, the appearance of a new technology actually promotes further improvements in the old one, as well as developments in completely new areas.
16. early fluorescent lamp
The fluorescent lamp is a good example.
When it was introduced, people thought the
incandescent light bulb would be put out
business. After all, the fluorescent
more light with less wattage.

There you sit, staring at your calendar. Six months ago, you agreed to give a presentation that's now only 6 weeks away. The first stirrings of panic are beginning to churn your stomach because you haven't written one word of your script or even thought about your visuals. What's more, you don't know where to begin.

Oh sure, you set goals for the presentation—you know what you'd like to accomplish.

And you studied your audience—you know what ideas and appeals should tie their motivations to yours.

And along the way you even had a few ideas about how to develop those appeals. You jotted down a few sentences, put them in a file, then went back to your job.

But now what? You have words to write and visuals to prepare, but your mind has run smack into the biggest thought-blocking and action-stopping question of all: "How do I begin?"

And that question has triggered a slew of others: Do you write the script first? Or do you plan the

visuals? How do you write a script for a presentation? How do you plan the visuals? When you finally have a script and ideas for visuals, how do you bring them together? Soon, the questions have come full circle, and you're back to "How do I begin?"

One good way to begin is to relax and realize that preparing the script and visuals for a presentation isn't as hard as it might seem. Yes, there's work involved, maybe even some frustration. All creative effort is marked by peaks of enthusiasm and valleys of doubt.

But you'll get through the valleys and attain the peaks if you have a method to follow, a progressive series of steps to take—one at a time.

To begin, let's look at the questions raised above.

Which Comes First: Script or Visuals?

This question smacks of the old chicken-or-egg riddle. And like that riddle, it can't be answered—at least not without some qualifications. That's because the answer to both questions will always depend on which element you decide is more critical in the process of creation. So choose: Is it the Laced Wyandotte or the Grade A large egg? And decide: Are words more important to your presentation, or visuals?

Answer "visuals" if all you want to do is smile smugly while a projector shows dazzling details of your company's new gas-sipping Econocar-X. Your script need contain little more than cues to "smile broadly" and "beam proudly."

If, on the other hand, you want to explain the operation of the Econocar-X's fuel saving engine, start with a script and let that be the springboard for your visual treatment.

How Do You Write a Script?

With a pencil, pen, or typewriter. Or dictate it into a tape recorder. It doesn't really matter.

What's that? This wasn't the kind of advice you were looking for? You *know* there's more to it than that?

To produce an effective presentation, you must have a method for organizing your thoughts and your visuals.

Of course, there's more to writing a script than choosing a method for recording your thoughts. But not much. The reason for the above answer, with its slightly flippant tone, was to cut short any thought you might have that writing a script for a presentation has to be difficult.

Yes, if you were asked to write the screenplay for Hollywood's next box-office blockbuster, that would be difficult. And if publishers were imploring you to write the next record-shattering best-seller, that too would be difficult. But you don't have to write a screenplay or novel. All you have to do is write a presentation about a subject that's probably important to you already. Chances are you talk about this subject every day and think about it even more frequently. So to write a script, all you have to do is get this talking and thinking on paper.

Here's where method comes to the rescue. Writing a script for a presentation is a task that involves five steps (all of them relatively easy).

1. Review your objectives. This should take no more than 10 minutes. Simply go back to the notes you made when you first decided to accept (or initiate) the presentation you're working on. Review the thinking process that helped you identify your audiences and their motivations. This short review not only refreshes your memory, it warms up your analytical and creative faculties for the work to come.

2. Set your theme. The theme of a presentation is its underlying argument, the one point you're trying to prove. This theme should be expressed in a single, simple, declarative sentence; for example, "The Econocar-X car is the most fuel-efficient car on the road today." Or "Senator Takecharge is right for our times." Or "The Palm Beach Relief Fund needs your financial support."

Phrasing your theme as a single statement to be proved helps you in two ways: First, it separates the extraneous from the essential. The subject of your presentation no doubt has many aspects and angles, but not all of them are relevant to what you're trying to accomplish. Some, in fact, would probably detract from your argument. For example, if you were trying to prove that the Econocar-X is the most fuel-efficient car available today, you would only dilute your argument and confuse your audience if you started talking about the car's sun room, lush interiors, and ample trunk space. A theme helps avoid these distractions: It focuses your thinking.

Second, a theme also helps you in two later stages of the script-writing process. It helps you plan and evaluate your research, and it helps you outline your thoughts prior to writing.

Where does the theme come from? To be effective, it should spring from a synthesis of your objectives and your audience's motivations. If your objective is to convince people to buy Econocar cars, and if your audience's motivation is to save money by owning fuel-efficient vehicles, your theme must link these elements. You must *prove* to your audience that your best interests (Econocar car sales) and their best interests (less expensive transportation) are intertwined.

3. Research your subject. This is a step that established reporters and experienced writers never skip, but which first-time or part-time writers skip almost unfailingly. Professional writers know their ideas, opinions, and conclusions are only as strong as the details that support them. They know that it's facts, figures, examples, anecdotes, and quotes that give their writing substance and believability. That's why they often spend up to 80 percent of their time on a project just doing research. But for inexperienced writers, that percentage probably falls to the other end of the scale; they spend 20 percent of their time in research, 80 percent writing. And the product of such research-deficient writing is usually a string of generalizations and abstractions—empty words that put audiences to sleep.

It isn't that the experienced writers are smarter than their inexperienced counterparts. It's just that they're better storytellers. And they know that a good story is concrete and specific. Just look at bookstore best-seller lists for proof. Rarely do you find books of philosophy or other highly conceptual subjects at the top spots; instead you find novels or narrative accounts of actual events—stories filled with people, places, things: the concrete and the specific.

Of course, the inexperienced writer knows that details make for more interesting reading; it's just that he or she doesn't put this knowledge into practice. As mentioned earlier, when an individual is asked to put together a presentation, it usually deals with a subject the person is familiar with. And familiarity, it seems, breeds abstraction. When a person works with ideas, assumptions, and conclusions day after day, he or she usually thinks and talks about this material in highly conceptualized, abstract terms. There's nothing wrong with this, as long as the abstractions mean something specific to both speaker and listener. When a computer expert tells another computer expert he's ordering software for his hardware so he can get more output from his input using a floppy disc, he's saying something both will understand in a specific, concrete sense. But if he talks like that to an audience of advertising copywriters, he's likely to get a few yawns in his feedback.

So inexperienced writers have to remind themselves to get back to the basics—to facts, figures, quotes and examples. And the way to do this is through research.

Like any other discipline, research is most effective when undertaken in a definite sequence of steps. A good rule to follow is to move from general sources to more detailed sources.

The most general source you can begin with, of course, is your own storehouse of information. What do you know about the subject? And what facts, figures, and examples back up your knowledge, opinions, and conclusions?

If you're truly an expert in your presentation's subject matter, your research may stop after you've examined your knowledge and experience. But for most people, some outside information usually helps develop and round out their initial ideas. This sort of information can often be found in published materials—newspapers, magazines, books, annual reports, product brochures, catalogues, transcripts of speeches, and scripts for movies and audiovisual presentations.

Thorough research is the key to a solid script.

Putting Words in Your Mouth

Not everyone can write a presentation script. Some people lack the time; others lack the talent. But that doesn't mean these people have to pass by an opportunity to make a presentation.

Their solution is to hire an experienced free-lance writer.

Before you flip open your Yellow Pages to Writers–Free-lance, you should know what to look for in terms of experience.

That guy who writes your company's sales brochures may be extremely talented, and the same may be true for the woman down the street who just had a book of poetry published. But their experiences and successes in those specialized forms of writing don't necessarily mean they're capable of penning a lively and interesting presentation.

When you look for a writer to help you with a presentation, you should look for three attributes:

1. The writer should have experience writing material that's meant to be spoken. It takes one set of skills to write prose that will be printed on a page, another to write a narration that will be read aloud. Copy for print has its own rhythm and style, more free-flowing and expansive than that for the spoken word, with sentences that ebb and flow, making a point and then expanding it or modifying it, much as this sentence has done. But try to read a mouthful like that during a presentation. You'll be gasping for breath halfway through. That's why writing for presentations uses short, declarative sentences like the last three. So when you look for experience, look for someone who has written successful presentations. You want to sound like a speaker, not like someone reading from a press release.

2. If you plan to use visuals, you should also look for a writer who's had experience thinking visually. That means you want someone who can take your ideas and turn them into visual images that tell a story. Good audiovisual presentations aren't just a collection of words and visuals; they're words and visuals that work in conjunction with one another, that reinforce each other, that amplify each other. So look for a writer who can give you more than pretty pictures to put on the screen. Look for someone who knows how to convey thought through visuals.

3. One visual does not a thought make. That's another way of saying you want a writer who can develop visual *sequences*. Think of the last time you watched a documentary or even a filmed news report on television. What you were watching, even if you didn't think about it, was a story told through a very deliberate and definite sequence of images. You might have seen, for example, a long shot of smoke and ash billowing from Mt. St. Helens, followed by a closer aerial view of the mountain, followed by even closer aerial views of the devastation at the base of the mountain, followed by shots of survivors leaving the area, followed perhaps by an interview with one or more of the survivors. When it's written out like this, you can actually see the sequence in a visual story–a far-off view followed by increasingly closer views, ending with a close-up, personal view. When you give a presentation, you want the same sort of logic and continuity to mark the progression of your ideas. That's why you should look for a writer with experience in developing visual sequences.

If necessary, you may also have to conduct interviews with people who can clarify the meaning of material found in previous research, or comment on the significance of your findings, or open up an entirely new area of investigation.

One area of research often overlooked by the inexperienced writer is personal observations. If you were writing the script for the Econocar-X car, for example, you might read in a product brochure that although the car has a small, fuel-efficient engine, it still offers plenty of acceleration. So you take the car for a test drive and find it goes from 0 to 60 mph in 10 seconds. That's personal observation–a specific fact uncovered by you that you can work into your script.

4. Organize your information. Teachers of composition have summed up the entire process of organization with three simple words: Form follows content. In other words, the organization of your writing–whether it's a 7-minute presentation or a 700-page book–should grow out of the content gathered during research.

For you, this should be a liberating thought. It means there's no *one* way to effectively organize material. Rather, there are dozens of ways. The best way is the way that tells your story with greatest clarity and emphasis.

So you can forget about rules. Forget about those precise outlines with their Roman numerals and upper and lowercase letters. Forget all those pedagogic instructions about Introductions, Middles, and Conclusions. You're not taking a test, you're writing a script. Release your creativity.

Do you feel a little more relaxed about the process of organizing your presentation? Good. That's important. You want your presentation to sound like a conversation–one person talking with another–not a lecture with its first, second, and third points.

So let's get down to business. You're trying to prove something, remember? You want people to accept your ideas–your theme–as true. And the best way to accomplish this is to involve your audience in the presentation.

One of the more effective ways to generate audience involvement is to follow this all-purpose organizing scheme:

Get your audience's attention.
To do this, put a startling fact, a dramatic example, or some other arresting piece of information right at the beginning of your presentation. Remember, before your presentation begins, people in your audience are going to be thinking countless other thoughts–about what the last presenter said, about the color of your suit or dress, about the work they left back at the office, about what they're going to have for lunch. The first thing you have to do with your presentation is stop all these extraneous thoughts and focus your audience's attention on you and your presentation.

Here's one way you could do this if you were organizing material for the Econocar car presentation: You might start with material related to the projected price of gasoline a year from now, 5 years from now, 10 years from now.

Tell the audience members why they should care. Once you gain an audience's attention, you have to tell them why they should continue to listen. So it's at this point in your organization that you insert material directly related to their motivations.

To continue with our Econocar car example, you might relate projected gasoline prices to the average miles driven in a year. Then you could ask a series of questions, addressed to members of the audience: "Are you prepared to pay these prices? To devote up to 10 percent or more of your income to transportation? Or perhaps to get rid of your car? Or are you more interested in cutting your gasoline costs by driving a car built for the 1980's and beyond?"

Questions such as these tie your presentation directly to the concerns of the audience. It makes them eager to hear your arguments.

There are many other ways, of course, to generate this sort of audience involvement. Your job is to find an approach that links audience concerns to the thrust of your argument.

Give them proof. It's at this point in your organization that you assemble the facts and figures you'll use to prove your theme. This is a matter of anticipating—and answering—questions that might occur to your audience. For example, how can an Econocar car save on gas? How much gas does it save? How does it save this gas? How is it different from other cars? How much better off will the average audience member be with an Econocar car?

Put yourself in a seat in your audience, then consider what sort of questions would be going through your mind. When you've listed them, marshal your facts, figures, and examples so they supply clear and emphatic answers.

Restate your theme and advance your conclusions. Once your major arguments have been made, restate your theme and the main points of your proof. This, of course, should be an artful presentation of the material, not just a mechanical rehashing of previous information. That means fresh language, perhaps supported with facts or quotes not used in your initial arguments.

Urge them to action. This section of your organization ties back to your communications objective—your statement of behavior change. What do you want your audience to do now that you've presented your arguments and support? Buy, sell, vote, pledge? Whatever it is, here's where you tell them what *you* want.

Filling in the content for this organizational scheme can be accomplished in any number of ways. If you want, you can develop and outline (but forget the Roman numerals, please; just write out a list of "points to be made.") Or you can jot down your main thoughts on 3-by-5-inch cards and shuffle them around until you're satisfied with the order of your arguments. A variation of this latter method is to use a planning board—a bulletin board or similar large board with several long plastic sleeves attached—on which you organize your cards according to the major sequences of your presentation. You can also write a letter to yourself in which you discuss the major points of your presentation. Or you can talk out your presentation with a colleague, making notes of the sequences in which your ideas seem to work best. Or you can use your imagination and develop a system of your own.

The point is: Organizing your material should be enjoyable, a problem-solving task similar to completing a jigsaw puzzle. So don't get hung up on rules or techniques. Let your method of organizing reflect your thnking.

5. Write your script. If you've followed the previous steps, you should, by now, be itching to write. Your mind is probably brimming with ideas; perhaps sentences and sequences have already started to write themselves. So give your creative energies their release and get your ideas down.

It should be so easy, you say. When you try to write, you bleed words. As you sit at your desk, pencil in hand, mind as blank as a freshly washed chalkboard, you begin to think, "It wouldn't be all that bad to get the flu. At least then people would sympathize."

Well, if this is a picture of you—if you're one of those people who can't write two words without crossing out one—you should know you're going about it the wrong way. Your trouble is you're trying to write and edit at the same time, and that's an almost impossible feat.

The secret to fluent writing is to make it a two-step process. In the first step you write a rough draft, the rougher the better; after all who's going to read it but you. Just write. Keep the pen or pencil moving over the page, the typewriter clacking. Or speak your thoughts into a tape recorder (best-selling author Sidney Sheldon uses this method to produce his books, so why can't you use it to produce a script?). Just forget about getting critical. Stop second-guessing your choice of words or the construction of your sentences. Just keep piling up the words.

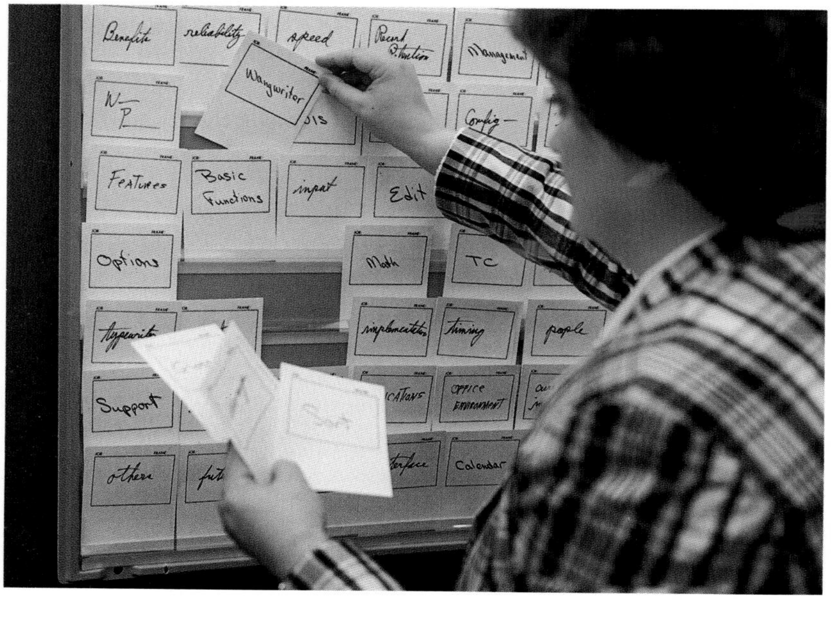

A planning board offers an easy and effective way to organize your thoughts.

Typing the Final Draft

Have you ever caught a glimpse of a television newscaster's script as he or she stacked it up at the end of a broadcast? If you have you probably noticed the copy ran only halfway across the page. This sort of format allows room to write visual directions and cues alongside the copy.

The final draft of your presentation script also should be typed following this two-column format. In the left-hand column, type your visual descriptions (see illustration). In the right-hand column, type your narrative.

This sort of format makes it easier for you to plan the integration of copy and visuals. It also assures precise coordination if you plan to have a projectionist advance slides or operate motion picture projectors during your presentation.

To make your script easier to read when you're on the podium, have it typed in orator type style (or any other larger-than-normal type style). Also, have the typist keep your lines to a maximum of 30 characters. Anything beyond this length can increase the difficulty of reading.

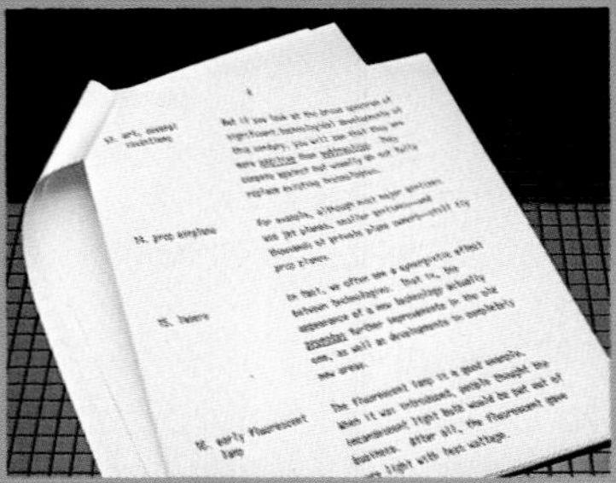

Since your eyes will be moving constantly from page to audience, it's also a good idea to highlight key words. This will make it much easier for you to find your place when you return your eyes to the page.

When you're through, you have the rough first draft of your script. And that brings you to step two—revision. Here's where you get critical, where you decide if you've used the right word in the right place, if your arguments are organized in the most effective order, if your transitions from idea to idea and paragraph to paragraph are smooth, if the overall presentation "makes sense." So make your changes. Scratch out sentences or paragraphs. Rewrite others. Insert or delete words. Use scissors and tape, rearrange paragraphs or pages.

One factor to consider as you revise is that you're writing for the ear, not the eye. So keep your sentences short and simple. Your audience will have a difficult time mentally sorting out lengthy sentences with convoluted phrasings. Also be aware of widely separated pronouns and antecedents. They're usually easy to link in a written sentence, but that's not always true when a sentence is spoken. Especially be alert to the pronoun "it." For a listener trying to sort out a multitude of ideas, "it" can be a source of endless confusion. So don't be afraid to repeat key words or phrases. This sort of repetition is often frowned upon in composition classes, but when you're writing for the ear, repetition is better than confusion.

After you've revised your script, have it retyped. (See example on page 96.) Then take an additional step. Get a tape recorder and read your script as if you were making a presentation. Pause where you would pause, emphasize where you would emphasize. Make it sound as polished as you can. Then, with the script in front of you, replay the tape. Put yourself in your audience and consider: Are you making your points clearly? Are you stumbling over difficult-to-pronounce words or awkward phrases? Are some of your sentences vague? Does the presentation move from section to section smoothly? Wherever you answer "no" to one of these questions, mark the script. Then go back and rework the material. If you have time–and you should allow yourself time–repeat the reading/listening/editing process until the script sounds as smooth, tight, and emphatic as you can make it. And then put your editing pencil away. You have other work to do.

How Do You Prepare Your Visuals?

Most people find it comparatively easy to plan their visual sequences. This may be because of the impact of television and movies on our lives, or it could be that most people just find it a lot easier to think in images. Ask people to think about something restful and serene and immediately they're conjuring up visions of warm sand and ocean spray or cool breezes blowing through the leaves over a mountaintop retreat. No one runs through a vocabulary list consisting of words such as placid, relaxing, or halcyon, not even the most devoted crossword puzzle fan. Images seem to be our natural way of thinking; we add words–labels–to our images to make thinking and communication more efficient and effective.

No one knows what prompted an ancient Chinese proverb-coiner to write that "One picture was worth more than 10,000 words," or how he even arrived at that figure. (And did he use a picture to express it?) Maybe he attended one too many presentations where a venerable

Art for Clarity's Sake

The caution raised about shooting your own slides if you're an inexperienced photographer also applies to creating your own artwork. Illustrations, charts, graphs, and typography to be used in a slide presentation must be created within a very definite framework. If this framework is ignored, you'll wind up with slide images that bleed into the slide mounts or slides with images so small that legibility is affected.

The best approach to take when you need art slides is to find an illustrator or graphic designer who's familiar with the requirements of slide photography.

Most producers develop a script by starting with the message. But sometimes starting with visuals can be just as effective.

speaker rambled on while a vulnerable audience endured inscrutably. The essence of this proverb, though, is well worth remembering when you're preparing for your presentation. Visuals may not be exchanged for words at the rate of 10,000 to 1, but they sure can save you a lot of time and breath.

To make your visuals as effective as possible, you should go through three steps:

1. Plan your sequences. As you were researching material for your script, you also should have been searching for visual support for your theme. This support could be photographic subjects; artwork that could be reproduced; ideas for charts, graphs, or graphics; and words or phrases that might be converted into type slides.

With notes on these visual possibilities before you, work your way through your script, asking yourself, "What sort of visual best illustrates, emphasizes, or reinforces the point being made in each sequence?" (As you gain experience in scriptwriting, you'll find

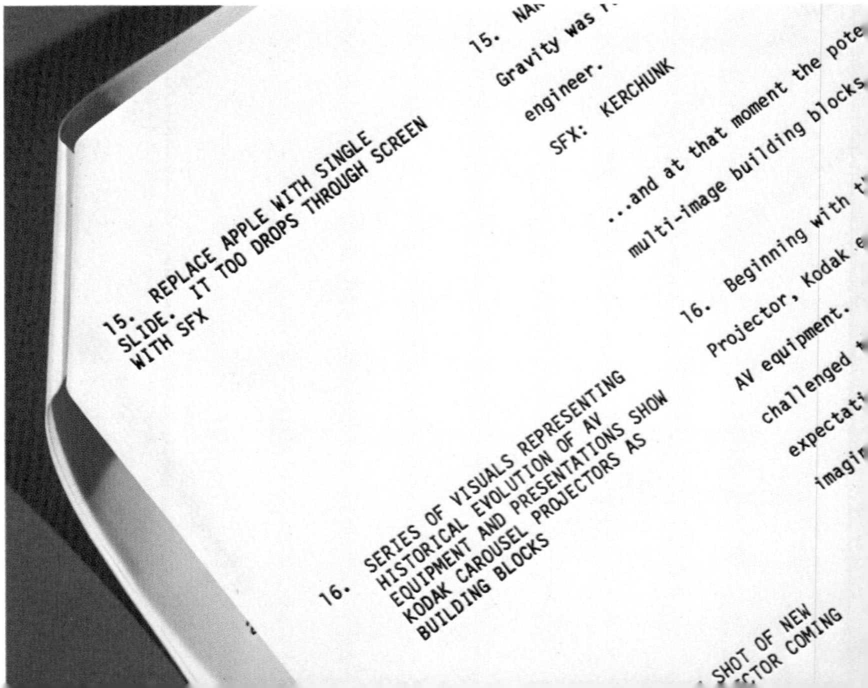

You can plan your visual sequences on a storyboard or briefly describe them in the left-hand column of your script.

yourself asking another question: "What sort of visuals can I use to replace words in a sequence?" When you get to that point, consider yourself a pro.)

Once you've found the visuals to integrate with your words, describe them briefly in the left-hand column of the script. Another way to proceed with this sort of visual planning is to sketch or describe your visuals on the cards in your planning board or on a storyboard. (See illustration.)

2. Shoot your slides. This book doesn't deal with the steps and techniques involved in shooting and processing slides. The best we can give is a rule of thumb: If you've never shot photographic slides or duplicated artwork or graphics, find a professional photographer who has. If you have some experience with a camera, decide what you can handle competently, then find an experienced photographer or studio to handle the rest. If you're planning to use film sequences, hire an experienced film producer. In short, don't jeopardize the success of your presentation by undertaking a task for which you have neither training nor experience.

This advice, of course, is for the short run. If you think you'll be making a number of presentations over the years, you may find it worth your while to learn how to shoot acceptable slides.

If you have to—or prefer to—work with a professional photographer, consider the following suggestions:

Use a photographer with experience in your medium. Shooting slides for an audiovisual presentation involves techniques different from those used for shooting portraits or product brochures. The audiovisual photographer must think in terms of sequence continuity—he or she must shoot a scene so it "develops" in stages. The audiovisual photographer must also be able to shoot on location, working under a wide variety of circumstances. He or she must also be able to work quickly—setting up, shooting, and moving on to the next location with a minimum of fuss and confusion. So if you're going to use a photographer—either from your organization or from an outside studio—make sure he or she is familiar with the audiovisual medium. If not, you may find yourself doing everything but setting the aperture opening and snapping the shutter.

Give your photographer complete instructions. Don't just hand a photographer a script or a storyboard and then hope he or she understands what you're trying to accomplish. Discuss your presentation with the photographer. Explain the mood you're trying to create, the emphasis you're trying to achieve, the details you want highlighted. In short, make the photographer a partner in the creative process. The results will repay your effort.

Ask for a variety of angles, distances, viewpoints. This suggestion accomplishes two things. First, it acknowledges that there are a number of ways to shoot a sequence, and the way you've suggested may not be the most effective one. To allow for this possibility, tell the photographer to expand on your suggestions, to let the photographic situation itself suggest shots other than those you've indicated. Second, additional shots of the key sequences of your presentation can often be used to illustrate your opening and closing segments, as well as

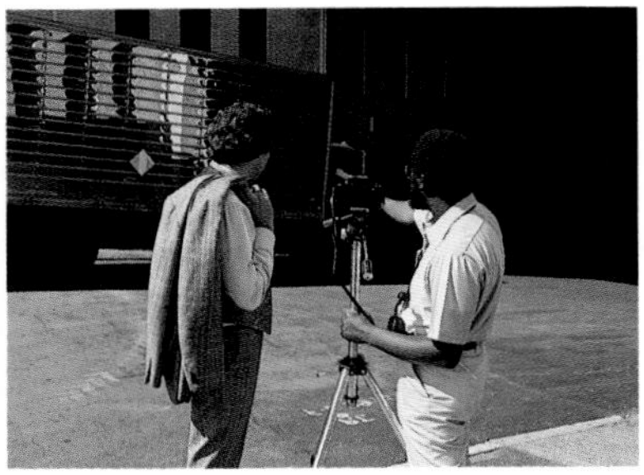

Don't expect a photographer to read your mind. Give explicit directions, but allow for the photographer's creativity.

other review or summary areas. So asking your photographer to shoot a variety of angles and viewpoints is a form of visual insurance: As you put the finishing touches on your presentation, you'll know you have the visuals to work with.

3. Organize your visuals.* Once photography is completed, you must edit and organize your visuals. The most efficient way to do this is with a large illuminator. Several different types of illuminators, from simple to sophisticated, are illustrated on page 99.

The first step in assembling your visuals is to edit out unacceptable slides. You can do this by holding the slides up to an illuminator or by projecting them using a stack-loading feeder. If you're working with more than two or three boxes of processed slides, it's a lot easier and faster to review your shots using a stack loader.

Next, group the remaining slides according to major sequences. Then, referring to your script, arrange the slides in each group so they illustrate and emphasize the key point of each sequence. Make the slides tell a story. And try to maintain continuity between individual slides and overall sequences. Don't, for example, jump from a long shot of a subject to an extreme close-up then back to a medium shot and then to another close-up. Your viewers wouldn't approach the subject in that sort of a progression, so the sequence of slides shouldn't either.

As you develop each sequence, keep moving the slides around. Throw out some and add others. Keep trying different arrangements until you find one that works to your liking. Repeat this creative tinkering and shifting until all your sequences are visualized.

With your slides organized, the next step is to mark your script at the exact point at which each slide is to appear during the presentation. One of the easiest ways to do this is to buy yourself a red ink stamp pad and a pencil with an unused eraser. Then simply ink the top of the eraser and mark the script over each word at which a slide change will be made. Later, when you're totally satisfied with your visual planning, you can number your slides and the corresponding red dots on the script. This simplifies loading trays and makes it easier to replace slides at a later date.

It's a lot easier to edit and organize slides when you have the right equipment–such as a light table and an illuminator.

The next, and last, step is to load your slides into trays. If you've never done this before, hold up your slide, top side up, then just turn it upside down and place it into the tray.

With your script written and your visuals developed, you're ready to move to the next step of preparation: Determining what equipment you'll need to produce and give your presentation.

*The content of this section pertains to the production of a basic slide presentation. If you're producing a multi-image presentation, we suggest you read *Images, Images, Images–The Book of Programmed Multi-Image Production*. It provides a more detailed description of the techniques and steps required to plan multi-image sequences.

How Many Slides Will Your Presentation Require?

This is one of the questions you can think about for hours and never come up with an approximate answer. The reason: too many variables.

First of all, realize that the equipment you select to use for your presentation will put certain limitations on you. If you're using a single slide projector or a desk-top unit, you're limited to either 80 or 140 slides, depending on the capacity of the tray you select. If you're using two projectors, double those figures; triple them for three projectors.

(Of course, you can always increase the number of slides you can use by planning for mid-presentation tray changes. But that's not always practical during a presentation, and the procedure is best avoided.)

Another strictly mechanical consideration is the speed with which a projector can change slides. A KODAK EKTAGRAPHIC Projector, for example, can advance a slide in approximately 1 second. That's a pretty quick cut, faster in fact than you'd want to change slides for more than a few seconds during a presentation. But at least you know what your outer limits are.

Another factor to consider is the running length of your presentation. If you're giving a 10-minute presentation and you're using an 80-slide tray, simple arithmetic tells you not to plan too many sequences with rapid slide changes unless you compensate for this with sequences in which slides stay on the screen for 10 to 20 seconds.

All these factors add up to this: There's no ideal number of slides to use in a presentation. You can, however, in your planning, allow for these various considerations by observing the following guidelines:

1. If you're projecting photographic slides using a single projector, aim for a slide change about every 10 seconds. That means you'll be projecting between six to eight slides a minute, a pace that should maintain viewer interest.

2. If you're projecting slides containing graphs or charts, slow down the pace of the presentation. Remember, even though you keep these slides simple, the viewer still has to perform some analysis, and that usually requires slightly more time than needed just to take away a visual impression. Let your own common sense be your guide: See how long it takes you to absorb the information on the slide, then add a second or two (remember, you're going to be familiar with the material in the slide).

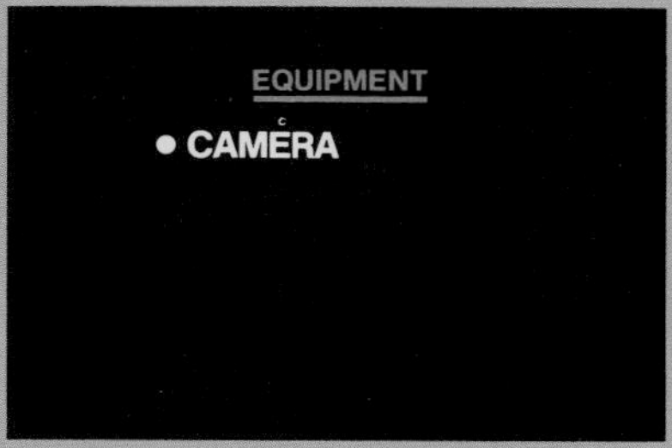
EQUIPMENT
• CAMERA

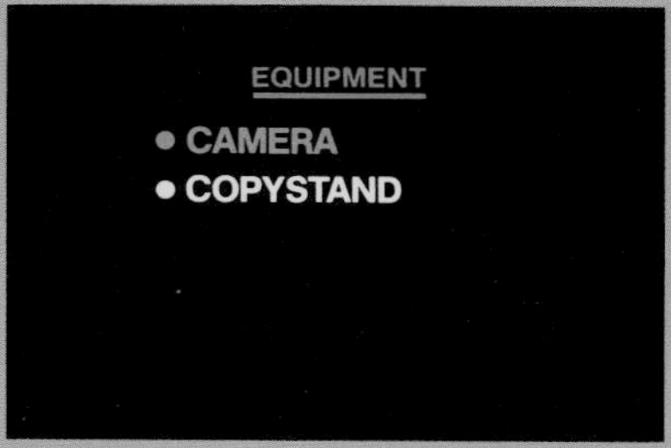
EQUIPMENT
• CAMERA
• COPYSTAND

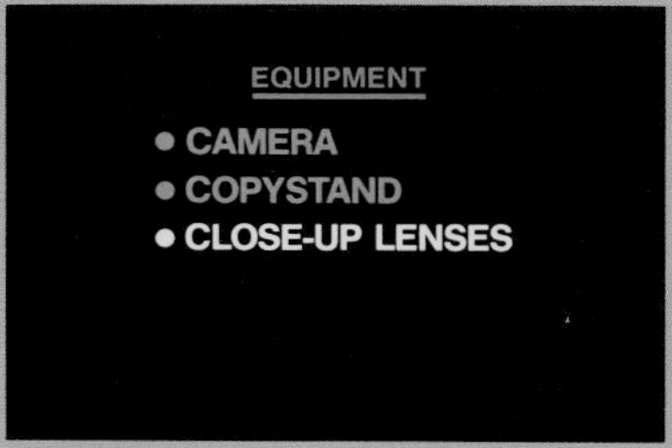
EQUIPMENT
• CAMERA
• COPYSTAND
• CLOSE-UP LENSES

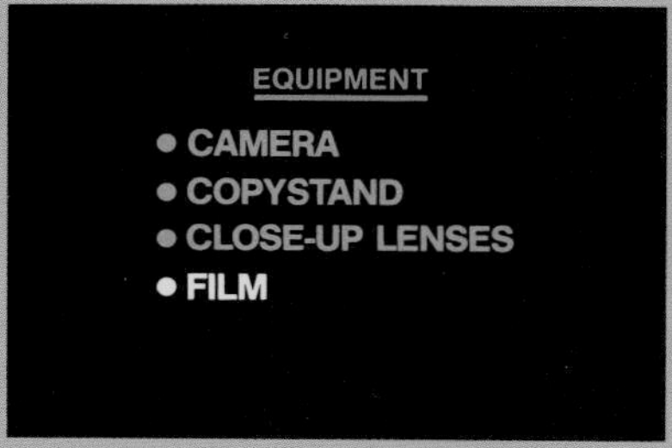
EQUIPMENT
• CAMERA
• COPYSTAND
• CLOSE-UP LENSES
• FILM

3. If the information in a graph or chart slide will require 20 seconds or more to read and understand, consider presenting that information in a sequence built on progressive disclosure. In such a sequence, one set of information is presented first, then another set is added to it. If needed, additional sets of data are added in the same way until the final chart or graph is constructed. (See illustration.) Such a method of presentation not only makes it easier for viewers to grasp the meaning and significance of the information, it also makes your presentation more interesting visually. Remember, every visual change renews attention and interest for your presentation, so the more slides you use, the less the chances of losing your audience.

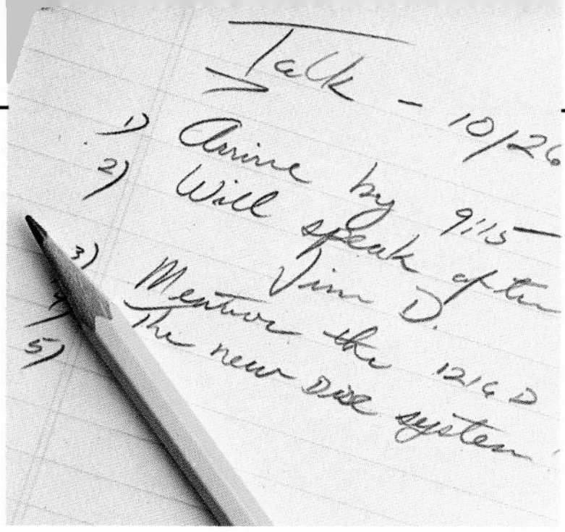

5 Script, Notes, or Memory?

There would be little need for a chapter such as this if we all possessed the presentation skills of Herman Kahn. Kahn, a futurist, the director of the Hudson Institute and an intellectual demigod often referred to as "a one-man think-tank," reportedly can make all-day presentations to an audience using only a minimum of notes and without ever repeating himself. The following day he can duplicate the presentation–or discuss the same subject matter from an entirely different viewpoint. He is so skilled a presenter, he often integrates slides into what otherwise seem to be extemporaneous performances.

These facts point to one conclusion: There is indeed a script for Kahn's presentations, only it isn't written on script pages or note cards. Instead, his script for a particular presentation is etched in his mind; he doesn't need to read, he only has to think it.

Unfortunately, few of us are capable of such mental feats. We may possess powerful intellects and strong memories, but once we stand before an audience we often find our performances hampered by anxiety. So rather than trust our presentation's success to memory or extemporaneous thought, we rely on a script, notes, or a thoroughly rehearsed patter.

And that prompts a question: Which approach is best for you?

The answer depends on two factors:

The type of presentation. Presentations, being of many types, have different types of requirements. Some presentations, such as a television talk show appearance, require you to speak spontaneously, in a conversational style. Other presentations, such as a major speech dealing with critical subject matter, usually require a written text. And there are still other presentations in which the choice of notes, script, or memory is entirely up to you.

The following suggestions should help you decide which approach is best for you:

Use a Written Script—When

• your subject matter is so critical that a wrong word or phrase can affect meaning or interpretation. Such is the case when a government official announces or discusses a new policy that affects the actions of citizens; or when the chairman of a corporation explains to shareholders or security analysts the financial record of a corporation. In cases like these, meaning can't be left to an extemporaneous choice of words.

• your presentation consists of fully integrated audio and visual. If you're making a slide, multimedia, or multi-image presentation, slide changes must be precisely coordinated with word cues. The only way to achieve this sort of harmonious audio and visual integration is to work with a script. If you're making the presentation alone, you'll have to know at what words to advance your slides. If you're working with a projectionist, he or she will have to be following your talk with a script in hand.

Rely On a Rehearsed Pattern—When

• you're making a presentation at an exhibit or a demonstration. These presentations are supposed to look spontaneous (even though most people realize that they're as well rehearsed as a Broadway play). The presenter should be as fully involved with the audience as possible, talking to them, watching their responses, adjusting his or her manner and delivery accordingly. You can't achieve this kind of spontaneity if you're holding a script in your hands or fumbling with notes.

• you're making a television appearance. When people watch a television presentation, whether it's part of a talk show or a locally produced public service program, they expect to hear a conversation, not a rehearsed performance. If they see a presenter reading from notes or a script, they'll quickly lose interest and switch to another channel (that's always your competition when you appear on TV). This puts a burden on the presenter: He or she must become thoroughly familiar with the material to be discussed, memorizing key facts and figures, developing examples and anecdotes when appropriate, even rehearsing the delivery of critical explanations if important.

Use Notes—When

• your presentation is to have an informal tone. If, for example, you're making an after-dinner presentation at an athletic banquet or an awards ceremony, you'll want to appear casual and conversational, even though your presentation has a definite structure. The best way to combine both structure and informality is by using notes. The notes keep you on track and remind you of the key points you want to make at each major section of your talk, but they also allow you to phrase these points in your own words—or to digress now and then when you see particular points heighten the interest of your audience.

Personal preference. Notes aren't inherently better than a script, and a script shouldn't necessarily be preferred over memory. If the type of presentation doesn't require you to use a particular method of recording your thoughts, then the choice is strictly one of personal preference. Which method are you more comfortable with? Some presenters, especially those with little experience, turn almost automatically to a fully written script. Those pages, which contain every word they plan to say, give them a sense of security. Other, more experienced presenters find that a script cramps their style, making them seem stilted and artificial. They prefer a few note cards or rely solely on memory for the order and content of their key points. (Several mnemonic techniques are especially suited for use by presenters who want to memorize the structure and content of their presentations. Their use is explained in almost all books on memory development.)

One effective approach to this kind of preparation is that used by many experienced speakers. These people usually prepare for their presentations by writing a full script (or having one written). This script gives them all the information, examples, and anecdotes they need to make their presentation. They then turn key words or phrases from this script into a set of note cards. They rehearse using the note cards–often taping their efforts–then compare their performances with the original script. If they feel it necessary, they add to or expand their notes. They'll also read the original script several times before their actual presentation. When they rehearse, however, they always rely on their notes. (If they want to commit the script to memory, they make a list of key words or phrases, then memorize them.)

This approach works because it fosters repeated reviews of the presentation material. The presenter becomes thoroughly familiar with the presentation material while developing or reviewing a full script. Much of this information, of course, is automatically stored in memory. When the script is then converted into note cards or a list of key words, it is further embedded in the presenter's memory. Later, the notes or key words serve as memory joggers; they remind the presenter of information he or she is by now totally familiar with.

This, of course, is the same process all of us use when we remember and retell a joke. When we first hear a joke, we don't copy it down word for word, then try to commit it to memory. We just remember the highlights of the buildup and punch line. When we retell the joke, we trust our memory to provide the situation and structure and our intelligence and creativity to fill in the gaps.

6 Preparations That Consider Your Audience

Sometime during your initial preparations you have to take a step away from your objectives, theme, script, and visuals and focus your attention on your audience. Their frame of mind before and during your presentation plays a large part in their acceptance or rejection of you and your message. So it's in your best interests to make sure the environment and circumstances surrounding your presentation create an overall atmosphere of comfort and relaxation.

Creating the ideal environment for your presentation may be a matter that's beyond your control.

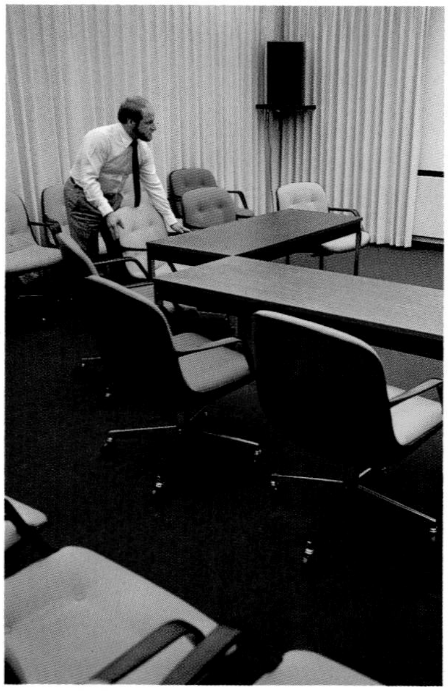

That's often the case when you're making a presentation in a client's conference room or a large hall at a trade show or convention. To prepare for these situations, find out in advance what sort of setup you'll be working in and then, if necessary, adapt your presentation to the environment. If, for example, it's mid-August and you learn the presentation site isn't air-conditioned, find some way to shorten your presentation. You might also shorten your presentation if you discover that people have to stand rather than sit while you talk.

On the other hand, if you or your organization is in control, plan to establish the most ideal conditions you can. Establishing these conditions requires consideration be given to three critical factors: seating, temperature, and acoustics.

Seating

All too often seating is given only a passing thought. If a presentation is to take place in a conference room, chairs are arranged around a table. If the presentation will be in a hall, folding chairs are arranged in a theatre pattern.

When planning your presentation site, make sure you create a comfortable environment conducive to communication.

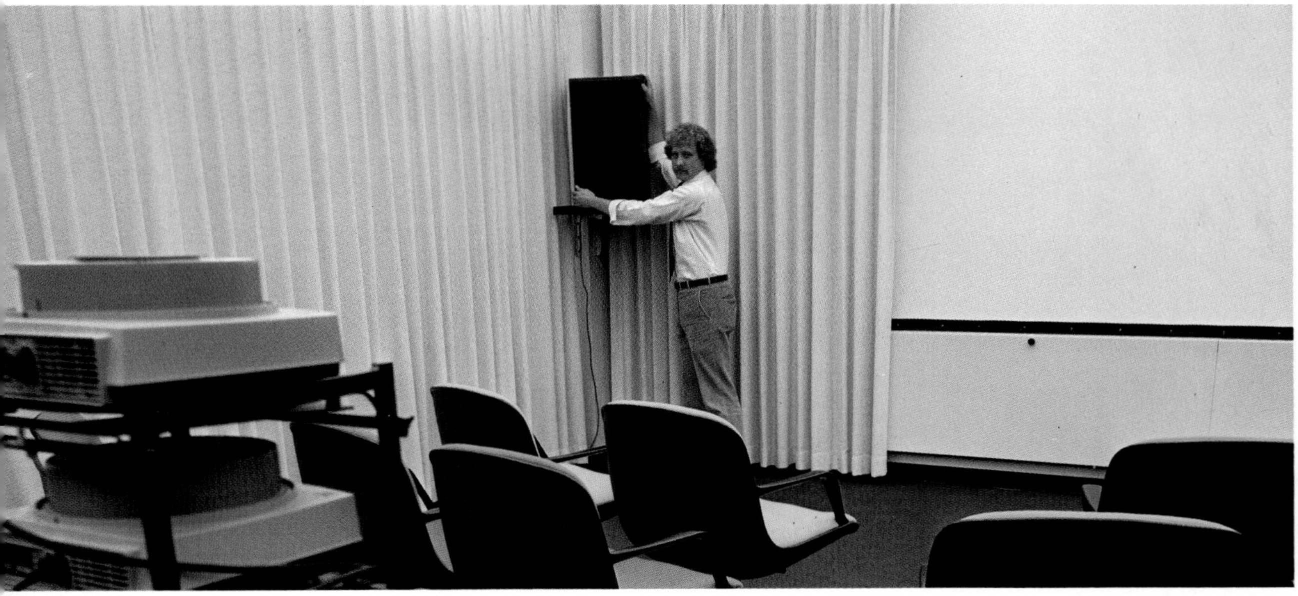

This kind of superficial planning ignores the fact that arrangements that suffice for strictly oral presentations may be totally unacceptable when visuals form an integral part of the performance.

You can plan effective seating patterns for your presentation by following these guidelines:

1. Outline your effective viewing area. No matter what type of room you make your presentation in, it's going to contain "dead" areas–sections of the room from which it's impossible to see your visuals clearly. The dimensions and location of these dead areas will depend to some extent on the type of screen you use to make your presentation. (Obviously, if you're using a tabletop presentation unit, you can bypass these preparations.)

There are three basic types of screen surfaces:

Matte screens diffuse light evenly in all directions. Images on matte screen appear almost equally bright at any normal viewing angle.

Lenticular screens reject light coming from above or from either side, providing excellent control of ambient light. Many lenticular screens also provide an image three or four times as bright as a matte screen.

Beaded screens reflect light toward their source, making them useful in long, narrow rooms or other locations where viewers will be close to the projection beam. They concentrate light, producing a very bright image (up to four times the brightness of that from a matte screen) but only in a restricted viewing area.

Figure 1

This is the best seating arrangement in a long, narrow room. A beaded screen or other narrow-angle screen is best in this situation.

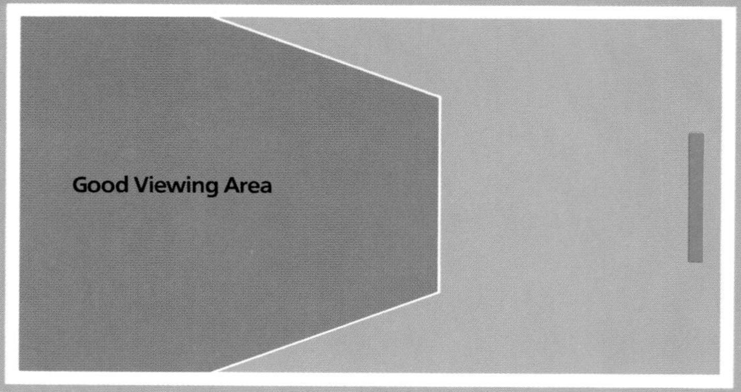

Figure 2

In a square room, a matte or lenticular screen offers a wider viewing angle.

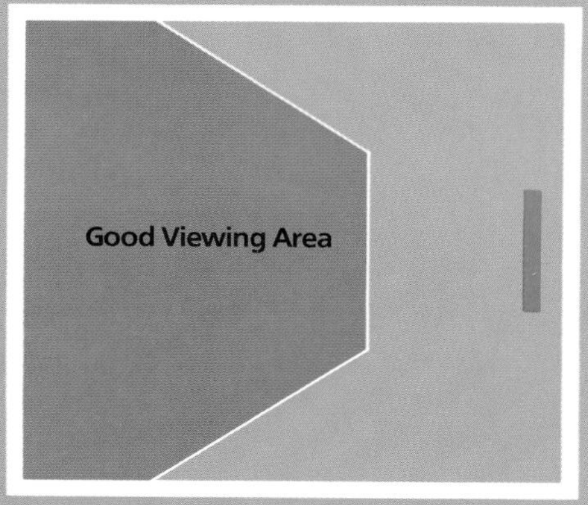

Figure 3

You can seat more people in a square room if you project your images diagonally. A slightly larger screen may be needed because of the greater maximum viewing distance.

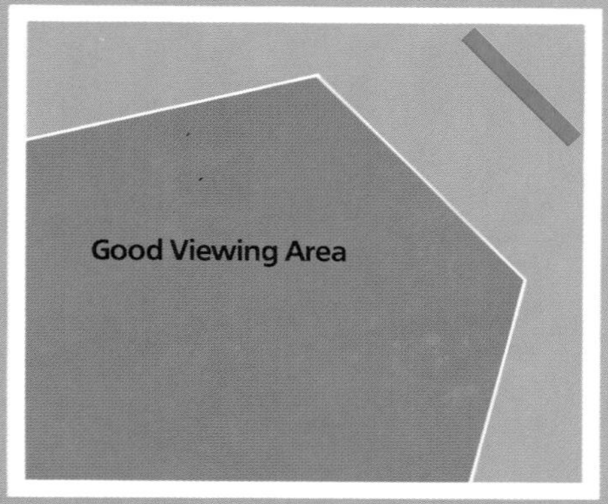

Taking these qualities of the various screen types into consideration, we can make the following broad statements about effective viewing area:

- In a long, narrow room (more than 1½ times longer than it is wide), the best arrangement is one similar to that pictured in Figure 1. A beaded screen or similar narrow-angle screen is your best choice if stray light can be controlled.

- In a room that's close to square, you'll be better off using a matte or lenticular screen. These screens offer a wider viewing angle, giving you a more effective viewing area. See Figure 2.

- You can increase your effective viewing area in a nearly square room by using a diagonally oriented screen and seating pattern, as shown in Figure 3. A slightly larger screen may be needed because of the greater maximum viewing distance.

If you'd like to plan your seating area more precisely, you can use the following formula to make a diagram. From each side of your screen, measure a distance equal to one third of the screen width.

From these points on the screen, draw lines toward the side walls according to the following angles:

- 90 degrees if you're using a matte screen for front projection;

- 60 degrees if you're using a lenticular screen for front projection;

- 50 degrees if you're using a beaded screen for front projection or one of the more popular rear-projection screen materials.

Now multiply your screen height by 2. Your answer tells you the minimum distance you should allow between your screen and the first row of seats.

Next multiply your screen height by 8. This answer tells you the maximum distance you should allow between the screen and the last row of seats.

Plot all of these lines and angles on a drawn-to-scale outline of your meeting area and you'll have precise boundaries of your effective viewing area.

2. Allow enough room for the people you expect. In general, if your presentation will be given in a large auditorium or meeting room, allow 5 to 6 square feet for each person expected. This space, of course, must be within the effective viewing area of your screen. This 5- to 6-square foot allowance, by the way, includes not only seating but also room for aisles.

If your presentation will be given in a conference room or a classroom with fixed seating, you must allow from 10 to 12 square feet of space for each person expected. This allowance includes not only space for seating and aisles but also for tables or desks.

By dividing the square footage of your effective viewing area by the suggested allowances, you'll end up with a fairly accurate estimate of the number of people who can attend your presentation. With this information, you can plan a comfortable seating pattern. See pages 166 and 167 for some of the more common seating arrangements.

Temperature control

Common sense is your best guide in this area. Your meeting area should be neither too cold nor too

For Professional Meeting Planners, Not Any Room Will Do

Most professional meeting planners take a leave-no-stones-unturned approach to finding and preparing a meeting site. They don't settle for a location just because it has the room for people and the power for equipment. They look for a site that can be turned into an effective presentation room–an environment where presenter and audience can get down to the business of sharing information.

This is especially true when a site is needed for a multi-image presentation. Since this type of presentation is usually made to large audiences, involves a great deal of equipment and a large screen area, and may feature more than one presenter, requirements and preparations tend to be specific and extensive.

Asked to describe an ideal multi-image presentation site, several experienced meeting planners listed the following criteria:

1. Ceiling heights of at least 20 feet, although an 18-foot ceiling would be acceptable.

2. No chandeliers or any other hanging fixtures or obstructions in the projection path.

3. A functional projection booth, preferably one that gives control of sound, stage lights, and projection equipment.

4. Plenty of room for equipment. Because of the sophistication of these presentations, planners look for the room and electrical power needed for an extensive array of equipment, including 35 mm and 16 mm motion picture projectors, anywhere from nine to more than 50 slide projectors, dissolve units and programmers, a tape playback unit, and other audio equipment.

5. A stage that is from 40 feet to 50 feet wide and from 8 feet to 12 feet deep. If dancers or other active performers are to be used as part of the presentation, planners prefer a stage depth of about 24 feet.

6. Screens that are at least 30 feet wide. A 10 by 30-foot screen is considered adequate.

7. Clean sight lines. Everyone in the audience–even those in the back corners of the seating area–must have an unobstructed view of the stage.

8. A loft area to hold "drops" if the presentation will require staging changes.

9. The flexibility to work with seating patterns. Seating requirements vary with the overall structure of the presentation. When the presentation is part of a banquet meeting, guests will be seated at round tables. Everyone is given plenty of room, so when the meal is over chairs can be adjusted to give an easy view of the stage. For this type of presentation, planners generally allow 16 square feet for each person. In a theatre-style presentation, the planners allow about 9 square feet for each person.

10. When the presentation requires it, planners look for ramps–or the space in which to construct ramps–that allow presenters to walk into the audience. This is especially important when the presentation requires that an intimate rapport develop between speaker and audience.

These requirements may seem unusually restrictive, but professional planners don't look at them that way. To these experienced people, specific requirements are one way to assure a successful presentation.

hot. But finding that median temperature at which most people will be comfortable will require some experimentation on your part. In choosing a temperature setting, remember to adjust the thermostat to a temperature just a little bit cooler than you might keep it if only you were to occupy the room. People in a closed meeting room generate heat, warming the area a few degrees once they've been seated for a while.

Also remember to provide good ventilation for the room. If smoking is going to be permitted, you'll also have to provide a source of fresh air.

Acoustics

For the most part, the acoustics of a room shouldn't be a problem. Once furniture, draperies, wall coverings, and people are brought into a room, its sound-absorbing and sound-reflecting qualities should be in effective balance. One factor you should take into consideration, however, is the possibility of distracting noises from an outside source. If a potential source of unwanted noise exists, take steps to eliminate it or reduce its intensity–if only for the length of your presentation.

You're Expected to Be Courteous

Your audience may be physically comfortable but emotionally distressed if you fail to show them personal consideration. In other words, an audience expects you to be a good host, someone who realizes that the audience's time, schedules, and priorities are as important as yours. You can show your consideration by adhering to two rules:

1. If you're in control of a presentation, always start on time. Unless something truly catastrophic has occurred, there's no excuse for delaying the start of your presentation. Last-minute preparations and checks should be completed 15 to 30 minutes before your audience arrives, not after they've taken their seats. Likewise, conversations with colleagues and friends should not take priority over an on-schedule start of your presentation. For people in the audience, especially those with busy schedules, nothing is more infuriating than watching a presenter fumble around with cords or projectors in what appears to be a last-minute scramble to get a presentation under way. To them, such a scene means the presenter didn't consider the pressures and demands they face. The result is an audience with negative feelings toward the presenter before the first word is spoken.

2. Stick to the scheduled time for your presentation. If your invitation or a program states the length of time you expect to talk, stick to that time frame. Run long and you risk the accomplishment of your goals. The final minutes of a presentation are critical, because it's during this period that you should be urging your audience to take a specific action. But if when that time arrives, your audience members are checking their watches and squirming in their seats–or worst of all, beginning to get up and leave–your presentation is teetering on the point of failure.

If you don't want an audience of clock-watchers, make it an unbreakable rule that you'll always end your presentation ahead of schedule rather than behind schedule. This simple precaution assures you of the goodwill of an audience. (It may also guarantee you a return engagement at some later date.)

3. Plan your presentation to stay within an audience's psychological and physical comfort limits. Yes, there are limits to how far any audience will go in waiting for a presenter to get to the point of his or her message. And that limit, communication researchers state, has been set by television viewing patterns. We have become a conditioned people. We like to have our information presented to us in 10- to 15-minute segments. After this point our bodies subconsciously begin to tell us it's time for a commercial break. Our concentration falls off, we begin to squirm a little in our seats. After a few minutes, we settle down again and refocus on the presentation material. The cycle is repeated again after about 30 minutes. At this point, however, concentration falls off even further and we become restless. It's as if our bodies are telling us the show's over, so we can get up and move around.

These observations would be little more than humorous comments on our society if they didn't also describe powerful forces you have to contend with. Of course, acknowledging them doesn't mean you must end all presentations at precisely 30 minutes after the hour. But you should plan your presentation to negate their influence. The following guidelines suggest ways to adapt your message to the average viewer's biological clock:

Try to keep your presentation from going beyond 30 minutes. Of course, as television has also taught us, a lot can be said in 30 to 60 seconds. But you have to have your audience's attention beforehand. Audiences have to be warmed up. They have to settle themselves down and mentally prepare themselves to be entertained or informed. That's why most top professional performers have lesser acts precede them on stage: To prepare the audience. In fact, these acts are called "warm-ups."

You too must take some time to warm up your audience to your message. How much time that will require depends to a large extent on your abilities as a presenter; the more dynamic and effective you are, the less time you'll need. For the most part, though, allow yourself at least 5 minutes to introduce and explain your message.

If you're planning a shorter presentation, take advantage of your audience's viewing habits and end it before their bodies begin signalling it's time for the 10-minute break.

If your presentation must run longer than 30 minutes, look for ways to introduce several changes of pace. Once again, this is merely a suggestion that you take advantage of the conditioned viewing habits of your audience. If they're going to get mentally and physically restless at 10- to 15-minute intervals, do something at these points to refocus their attention.

You can use a number of techniques to assure the continued attention of your audience:

- shift from your "live" presentation to a "canned" slide or film sequence;
- shift from the use of slides to the use of film;
- use more than one presenter, and shift responsibility for the narration from one to the other;
- shift from narration to a segment using just music and visuals.

These are just a few suggestions. Your own imagination can–and should–devise a technique that works bets with the goals and content of your presentation.

The length of your presentation–or presentation segments–must consider the activity patterns of your audience.

To Be a Good Presenter, First Be a Good Guest

Ed Larkin

"There's no secret to being a courteous presenter," says Ed Larkin. All it takes is common sense and effort.

Larkin should know. He's been booking speakers–and coaching them–for more than a dozen years, most recently as a partner in Speakers Guild Inc., of Sandwich, Massachusetts.

In this role, Larkin books speakers for *Fortune* 500 companies and for trade and professional associations throughout the world. A good part of his effort, he says, goes into helping sponsoring organizations to be good hosts. The remainder of his time is devoted to coaching his speakers to be good guests. Much of this work is built around a basic list of dos and don'ts he reviews with speakers, especially those who are new to the podium.

Larkin's guidelines cover three critical phases of preparation and performance: accepting an invitation, checking preparations, and making the presentation.

Accepting the Invitation

During this phase of preparation, Larkin advises speakers to gather information about the proposed presentation. It's also important, he says, to provide the sponsoring organization with information on the proposed topic and the speaker's qualifications.

1. "Learn as much about an audience as is possible," advises Larkin. This means asking for the usual demographic information–age, sex, educational background. "More important, though," says Larkin, is "to find out what the audience members do for a living. Find out what functions, divisions, or organizations they represent. If they're managers, find out at what level. This enables you to aim your presentation to the audience's background and interests."

Another way you can help yourself get a better feel for the audience and occasion for your presentation, says Larkin, is to ask to be put on the mailing list for all materials going to attendees.

2. "If you're going to share the podium with a number of other speakers," says Larkin, "find out who they are, what they're going to say, and who will speak before and after you." The organization sponsoring your presentation should be able to provide this information.

Larkin says such a request is a simple way to avoid redundancy. "One of the quickest ways to lose an audience," he adds, "is to cover the same subject matter, in the same way, as a previous speaker."

3. When requesting information from the sponsoring organization, also find out where in the program you're going to speak "If at all possible," advises Larkin, "avoid giving a serious presentation *after* a dinner. It's as good a guarantee of failure as you can get."

If you find that your no-nonsense presentation is scheduled for after dinner, ask the sponsoring organization if the agenda can be changed. (If you plan to give a presentation that's built around humor, don't worry. People don't mind being entertained after a meal, but a full stomach seems to discourage the mind's ability to ha ndle serious issues.)

If the program schedule can't be changed, make sure that your presentation won't begin until *after* all the dishes have been cleared away and the kitchen help has left the presentation room. "There's no tougher competition," says Larkin, "than the banging and clinking of dishes and tableware as they're dumped into trays."

4. Reciprocate. If possible, submit a brief outline of your presentation to the sponsoring organization. That information will help the organizers fit your message into the overall program.

Also provide background on yourself. In straightforward terms, tell who you are, what you do, what you've accomplished (if pertinent), and, most important, why you're qualified to make a presentation on your particular subject. Again, this information will help the organizers develop the total program. It also will help if promotional activities and publications are planned. If you have a black-and-white glossy photograph of yourself, send that along too.

Checking Preparations

This is the time of last-minute checks. It's also a time to check out your own mental preparedness.

1. Arrive early. "Don't ever be late for a presentation you're supposed to give," warns Larkin. "That's worse than being inconsiderate," he says. "That's being plain rude. When a speaker's late for a presentation, that means the audience is just sitting around with nothing to do. They're sure to be in a foul mood when you show up–provided they stick around at all."

When Larkin advises speakers to arrive early, he means to be at the presentation site at least an hour or two before the presentation is to begin. If you're traveling out of town to give your presentation, he advises you to plan to arrive at your destination the preceding evening. This advice is doubly important if your presentation is scheduled for the morning.

2. When you arrive early, you not only put the presentation organizers at ease, you also give yourself time to check out the presentation site. "You'll be a much better presenter if you make yourself comfortable," he says. "That means becoming familiar with the size of the room and with the seating. Stand at the podium and try to get a feel for the room as it'll be when the audience is there. Check out the microphone and the sound system. If you're unfamiliar with the microphone, find out how it works. Also find out how volume is to be controlled. And, if possible, ask for a sound volume check, or find out when the sound system will be checked."

These preparations allow you to step to the podium with confidence, ready to begin. And if you're confident, enthusiastic, and ready to go, this emotional tone will be transferred to your audience.

3. You wouldn't be human if you didn't experience a little nervousness and anxiety just before your presentation is to begin. That's why Larkin suggests you "try to get a few quiet moments alone before going on." If you can't get away from the head table or dais before your presentation, retreat into your mind for a few minutes. Whatever your approach, your goal is to calm yourself and collect your thoughts. You might wind up this miniretreat by giving yourself a positive suggestion of success.

Making the Presentation

Once your presentation is under way, remember you have an audience in front of you. Sure, you'll see them, but that's not enough. You have to put yourself in a seat in that audience; once you do, remind yourself of the Speaker's Golden Rule: Present unto others as you would have them present unto you.

1. Say what you have to say and then sit down. The most natural question at this point is, of course, how long should a presentation be? Larkin admits it's hard to set down any hard-and-fast rules to govern the length of a presentation. "My advice is to let the subject matter dictate the length of a presentation. That means don't try to pack an hour's worth of material into 20 minutes. That'll simply overwhelm an audience. On the other hand, don't try to stretch 20 minutes of material into an hour presentation. You'll only bore an audience."

Further complicating the length-of-presentation problem is the question of the presenter's ability and experience. "I usually tell an experienced speaker to limit a presentation to 45 minutes to an hour. And within this time there should be a period of questions and answers." With a less experienced presenter, an hour-long presentation might be a risky undertaking. It not only takes a considerable amount of information, but also a great deal of talent and ability, to keep an audience interested for an extended period of time.

2. Use common sense and good taste with humorous material. "Never," Larkin emphasizes, "use off-color material or ethnic jokes. And don't make fun of an audience's business or profession. Finally, don't use people at the head table or members of the audience as the butt of your jokes."

3. Larkin calls his last guideline the cardinal rule for all speakers: "Never run over your allotted time." Larkin has attended presentations where speakers have completely ignored the time limits set for their segments. The worst case he can recall is one in which a speaker talked without any regard for schedules while jittery members of the audience sat waiting to get on buses that were to take them to the airport. "The speaker didn't make many friends that day," Larkin recalls.

"If there's one rule of courtesy to remember and apply it's this one: Stay within your allotted time."

Larkin admits his suggestions won't necessarily win an audience over to your point of view. But by showing courtesy at the podium, you can win an audience's acceptance.

And that's a big part of a presenter's challenge.

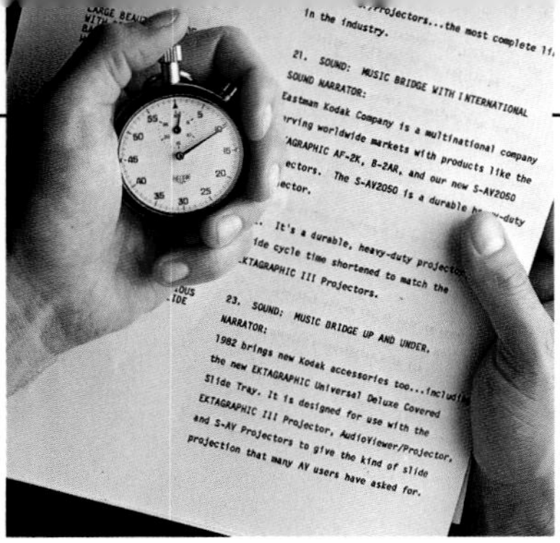

7 Practice Makes Perfect

People are always searching for ways to protect their investments. They want advice and strategies to protect their savings. They want devices to keep their houses safe and secure. They want undercoatings and surface waxes to protect the bodies of their cars.

So how about protection against presentation failure? Interested? You should be. After all, consider all the time, energy, and money you've invested in your presentation so far. If something should go wrong when you step before your audience, all that effort could be lost.

Naturally that's something you want to avoid, and one of the best ways to give yourself presentation protection is through rehearsal. Singers rehearse, musicians rehearse, comedians rehearse, actors rehearse, so why not someone who's about to make a presentation? Practice may not make perfect, but it should bring you close enough so that few in your audience know the difference.

So make this an ironclad rule: Rehearse your presentation once, twice, three times, even more—*before* you give it to an audience. Assume the working habits of the pros. It's sure to rub off on your performance.

There are several reasons why all this practice can make you a better presenter.

First of all, rehearsals give you an opportunity to refine your narrative and visual materials. For the most part, a rehearsal is the first chance you'll have to see and hear all the elements of your presentation working together. And more than likely you'll find that passages of your narrative, which seemed perfect when you originally wrote them, now seem wordy and awkward when integrated with your visuals. Or maybe you'll find that some of the slides you thought would emphasize a point now seem to miss the point instead. Make notes of these rough spots as you rehearse, then go back later and refine and polish these areas.

Rehearsals also give you a chance to become familiar with the equipment and setup you'll use during your presentation. Remember, your audience came to see and hear an expert; if they see a presenter performing a Buster Keaton routine with projectors and screen, it detracts from that image—and from your message. So, during your rehearsals, get

Make your mistakes and master your delivery before you face an audience. That's what rehearsals are for.

your hands on the equipment you'll be using. Set up the screen and projectors, load the trays, focus the lenses, test the sound system. You won't have time to learn the mechanics of these operations on the day of the presentation. (And don't use the excuse that you'll have an assistant to help you. What if your assistant should be sick that day, or late, or lost? What would you do then? Better to know how to use your presentation equipment. That's the image of an expert.)

After you've run through your rehearsals a number of times, you'll begin to appreciate another benefit of this practice: You'll find that you know your narrative better than you might have expected. This happens because the repeated rehearsals are etching a groove in your memory. Your ideas, arguments, facts, and examples have become part of your mental repertoire. You can recall and use this material just as easily and naturally as you recall information during the course of everyday conversations. When this absorption of material takes place, it serves as a major boost to your confidence. You realize you don't have to fear what some speech experts call the fear of breakdown–that nagging possibility that when you step before an audience your mind will go blank. Because of your rehearsals, that can't happen; your presentation is stored in your memory.

Rehearsals also provide another psychological boost to your confidence. After you've made your presentation a number of times–even though it's to an empty room–you begin to feel comfortable in the role of presenter. That, of course, is why actors rehearse–not just to memorize their lines, but to become accustomed to the character they're supposed to play. Rehearsals will allow this transformation to take place in you, too. After you've run through your presentation several times, you begin to see yourself as a presenter, not as an accountant, manager, or volunteer who's been asked to make a presentation. That difference in viewpoint might seem slight, but it's not. It's significant. If you regard the making of a presentation as an unnatural activity for you, you go before your audience with doubts and anxieties filling your mind. This sort of mental state is almost certain to inhibit your performance. On the other hand, if you can step before your audience comfortable in your role as a presenter, you'll feel and exhibit confidence—and your presentation will reflect that.

How to Organize a Rehearsal

You have to prepare to prepare. Rehearsals aren't sessions you begin on the spur of the moment, just because you have a spare 15 minutes on your calendar. You have to establish the right conditions, assemble the right equipment, and invite the right people. If you don't, while you won't be wasting your time, you won't be getting full benefit from your efforts either.

To run a business-like rehearsal, here's what you have to do:

1. Find an area that duplicates, as much as possible, the site of your presentation. If you're going to present a proposal in a conference room, find a conference room. If you're making a presentation at an equipment demonstration, try to find an area with a similar piece of equipment. If you're going to present your message in a large hall or ballroom . . . well, you're going to have to improvise here. Try to find as large a room as possible, one that will give you a sense of having to project your voice and personality to people sitting some distance from the podium. In looking for a rehearsal site, remember: You want to get yourself accustomed to—and comfortable with—the type of conditions you'll be working in. So, if you have to improvise, improvise as skillfully as possible. Don't just settle for whatever room happens to be available.

2. Use the same equipment you'll use in your presentation. That means just what it says—the same equipment. Not similar equipment or whatever equipment happens to be available, but the exact equipment you'll use the day of your presentation. This emphasis springs from the fact that no two pieces of equipment are exactly alike. They may be when they're manufactured, but after use they begin to develop mechanical idiosyncrasies of their own. The time to learn about those idiosyncrasies is during rehearsals, not on the day of your presentation. So assemble the equipment you'll need, rehearse with it, then take it with you. This approach eliminates another category of possible surprises.

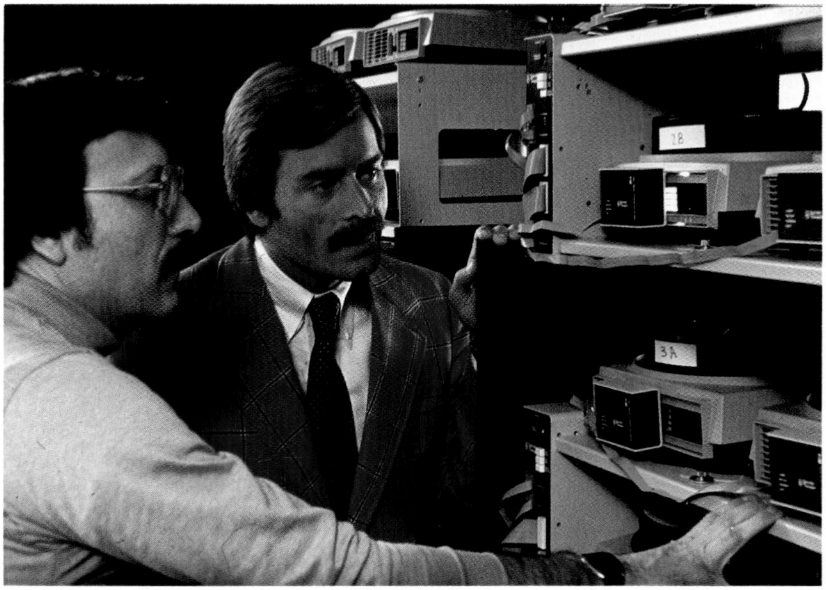

Rehearse with the equipment you'll use during the actual presentation.

Practice Not Only Makes Perfect, It Also Makes for Comfort

Producer Chris Korody tells his clients there are four critical reasons for rehearsing a presentation:

1. It gives presenters a chance to become familiar with their material.

2. It gives people who will be operating projectors and other equipment a chance to become familiar with their functions.

3. It enables presenter and presentation crew to mesh their efforts, giving the presentation what Korody calls "polish."

4. It allows presenters to establish "comfort levels."

The latter reason is the one most overlooked by inexperienced presenters. "Too many presenters think that once they know their words and their pacing that they're all set," claims Korody. "They seem to feel that time spent rehearsing their presentation alone is just as good as time spent up at the podium, in a setting that simulates actual presentation conditions."

All too often, unfortunately, that turns out to be a costly assumption. When it comes time for the actual presentation, the presenter becomes disoriented.

"All of a sudden," says Korody, "everything seems strange to the presenter. Spotlights may be shining into the presenter's eyes, leaving him unable to see the audience. His voice may sound different because it's amplified by the public address system and filling the presentation site. The light on the podium may not illuminate the script, or the podium itself may be too high or too low. When these things start to happen, the presenter begins to direct his attention to the environment and not to the presentation."

To avoid this sort of discombobulation, Korody insists that his clients plan on attending rehearsals. "Right at the outset of production," he says, "we emphasize that time must be set aside for rehearsals. In general, the more presenters involved and the more complex the presenter-to-media interaction, the more time we require for rehearsals."

When possible, Korody likes to set aside at least 1 day for what he calls "technical rehearsals." During this time the presentation crew runs through all the operations it must perform on the day of the presentation–erecting a stage or set, setting up equipment and running the actual presentation. If the presentation is going to be shown at multiple sites–as was his Datsun new car introduction (see page 38)–Korody will also have his crew run through tear-down and packing operations.

After the technical crew has become familiar with its routines, Korody schedules one or two days of dress rehearsals. During these sessions, presenters and technical crew run through a presentation as if an actual audience were watching.

"We have the presenters up at the podium so they can get used to the lights and so we can get sound levels on the microphones," he says. "We want them to be completely familiar with the presentation environment. Once they do, they'll feel more comfortable and will be able to concentrate on their material."

These sessions don't end the need for rehearsals, however. Korody likes to run through a presentation at the actual site. If this isn't possible, he at least likes to rehearse the more critical or more complicated segments of a presentation.

"There's no question about it," he says, "we like to have as much rehearsal time as possible."

And Korody wouldn't have it any other way. "The success and polish of a presentation," he says, "is directly related to the time spent in rehearsals."

3. Use the same projection setup you'll use at your presentation. If you're planning to use three projectors side by side, set them up that way during rehearsals. If you're planning to use the three projections stacked in a carrying rack, use this setup during rehearsals. The reason for this is similar to the reason given in Point 2: You don't want surprises on the day of your presentation. So become accustomed to your entire setup during rehearsals.

4. Make certain the right people attend your rehearsals. The right people are the ones who'll be working with you on the day of the presentation. Sorry, no substitutes allowed. Again, just as you have to be accustomed to your equipment and projector/screen setup, so, too, do you have to become accustomed to working with your assistants. (And they have to become accustomed to working with you.) On the day of the presentation, you'll all be working as a team, and teams must practice together. So when you line up your presentation team, be certain they're available not only for the presentation date, but also for all the rehearsal dates that precede it.

5. Schedule a dress rehearsal before a hand-picked audience. During this rehearsal, make your presentation as if you were before your true audience. Dress the way you'll dress on the day of the presentation. Stand or sit the way you'll stand or sit. Use your script or notes the way you plan to use them before your audience. Use your visuals and any other media you plan to use just the way you'll use them at the presentation. This full dress rehearsal should be as good as you and your assistants can make it, because you're going to have an audience critiquing your performance.

This audience should be made up of your colleagues and anyone else with an interest in your presentation. Their role will be to offer constructive criticisms of the performance—suggestions on ways the presentation might be improved.

To make this critique session successful, you have to set the right atmosphere. You don't want to hear polite but meaningless accolades, nor do you want people to approach the session with a find-ten-things-wrong-with-this-presentation attitude. Instead, you

It's helpful to rehearse before colleagues who can offer suggestions for further improvements in your presentation.

want helpful suggestions. Invite these suggestions, accept them cheerfully and eagerly, and thank your audience after the critique is over. Then go back to your office and, with your presentation team, evaluate the suggestions. Adapt those you find meaningful and practical; ignore the others. Then work these refinements into your presentation, thankful that you discovered them now, not later. Finally, rest assured–your presentation is probably as close to perfection as you can make it.

How Often?

From all that's been written, don't get the idea that weeks of endless rehearsals are all you'll need to guarantee a successful presentation. It doesn't work that way. In fact, rehearsals can reach a point of diminishing marginal returns. Your challenge is to determine where that point is.

In trying to schedule the "correct" number of rehearsals, keep this suggestion in mind: Rehearse to the point where you're familiar and comfortable with your material, but not to the point where you're beginning to sound stale. Athletic coaches wrestle with this problem of practice and training throughout their seasons. They want their athletes to be in top shape, well skilled and well drilled. But they can't push this kind of training too far. Their goal is to arrive at a competition with their athletes "peaked," full of energy, full of desire, and *eager* to play.

And that's how you should feel after your last rehearsal. You should be comfortable with and confident in your material, so comfortable and confident in fact that you're looking forward to stepping before your audience. Like a well-trained athlete, you should feel peaked, full of energy, brimming with desire, and eager to speak.

The following suggestions are meant to help you determine the number of rehearsals necessary to reach this point:

1. Try to schedule at least two rehearsals before your dress rehearsal. This may sound like a lot, but remember, your first rehearsal is going to be little more than a walk through your material. You'll be stopping and starting, perhaps backtracking, making notes, and adjusting equipment. This is what a first rehearsal is for–to find the rough spots and the kinks. So two or three preliminary rehearsals aren't too many. Rather, they're just a starting point, a minimum number.

2. Schedule at least one dress rehearsal. The reasons for this have already been covered. One additional point: Consider scheduling a second dress rehearsal if the first one went poorly, or if you've made major changes as a result of your audience critique.

3. When and where possible, schedule at least one rehearsal at your presentation site. Do this to acclimate yourself to the new surroundings. Examine the areas where you'll set up your projectors and screens. Find the electrical outlets. Stand at the podium or at the front of the room and let your eyes take in the seating pattern and the surroundings. As you talk, let your ears become accustomed to the room tones. All these little acts of familiarization will make you just a little bit more comfortable and confident when you finally stand before your audience. You'll feel like you belong there. And, indeed, you will.

mazda
R.S.V.P.
1981 Model Announcement Meeting
Dealership
City
Number of People Attending
Name/Title
SCHEDULE OF EVENTS
1981 Model Announcement Meeting
Reno, Nevada
September 28th & 29th, 1980

Promoting the Presentation

Remember Ron Hoff, the advertising exeuctive introduced in Chapter 1? He accepted an invitation to make a presentation, prepared his materials, flew from New York City to his engagement, then found his time, energy, and money had netted him an audience of five people.

Hoff considered his presentation a failure. But it wasn't a failure of his making. Rather, it was a failure brought about by ineffective promotion. Little, it seems, had been done to generate excitement and enthusiasm for Hoff's appearance. As a result, the turnout was disappointing, leaving Hoff feeling he had wasted his time.

If you don't want to experience similar feelings of disappointment, you must take time to promote your presentation–or to see that others promote it. Face the facts: Unless you're a celebrity with a large following, people probably aren't clamoring to hear you. You have to build interest in you and your ideas. You have to coax people to attend your presentation, you have to entice them, you have to persuade them that it'll be worth their time–and maybe money–to listen to what you have to say.

Many inexperienced presenters overlook this aspect of preparation as they concentrate on script, visuals, and equipment. Their thoughts are focused on themselves, their problems, and the countless details that must be attended to before they can step before an audience. At these times, promotion seems like a peripheral concern. But it's not. Without an interested and, ideally, an eager audience, all their scriptwriting, photography, and planning can amount to a case history in futility. Even the most dazzling presentation can't excite an empty hall.

Invitations to a presentation may take the form of a simple memo or a sophisticated advertising campaign.

The amount of promotion needed to build an audience depends for the most part on the type of presentation you're giving.

A presentation to employees usually requires little more than a memo explaining purpose and place, to be sent to managers or supervisors. Posters highlighting the purpose of the presentation, posted on bulletin boards, are another way to build employee attendance.

A sales demonstration to a prospect can be promoted in a number of ways. The easiest–and usually most effective–is a personal invitation made during an initial sales call. A follow-up letter can be used to generate even greater interest in the presentation. You can also use a letter–or a series of letters–to extend the initial invitation. This is an effective promotional tactic when your presentation is aimed at a class of customers rather than a specific customer. Of course, the letter or letters used in this type of promotion must contain some effective selling and appeals, as well as information on time and place.

More elaborate presentations, such as distributor sales meetings, usually require more extensive promotion. Distributors, after all, don't have to attend your presentations. In fact, your presentation may conflict with other events or priorities on their calendars. In situations like these, you have to go all out to entice people to attend. You have to convince them that your message is not only something they want to hear, but, more emphatically, something they can't afford to miss. To do this, you'll have to use high-powered promotional techniques such as "teaser" campaigns, intriguing but informative notices developed to build interest and curiosity in your presentation. If this sort of campaign would help build an audience for your presentation, ask for help from your organization's sales promotion department or from an agency that specializes in sales promotion activities.

Workshops and lectures–other than those for employees–are promoted extensively, but usually in more sedate ways. Brochures explaining the content and time of the presentation may be prepared and mailed to people who have demonstrated an interest in your subject matter. In addition, press

Don't leave the promotion of your presentation to chance. Plan your publicity with the help of a professional.

releases may be sent to newsletters or magazines aimed at key audience groups. If appropriate, ads promoting the presentation may be inserted in these publications.

Presentations made at major conferences may require large-scale and well-organized publicity and promotion campaigns. These campaigns are usually planned and directed by public relations or public information departments. Many different vehicles of promotion may be used: prepresentation news releases announcing the subject, time, and place of the presentation, plus biographical details on the presenter; invitations to key press representatives and to influential people with an interest in the subject matter; press interviews with the presenter, if appropriate. Following the presentation, a summary news release may be sent out, highlighting the main points of the presentation.

An effort of this magnitude, of course, requires the involvement of experts in publicity and promotion. As already mentioned, these experts can be found at public relations and sales promotion departments or agencies. In addition, if you're part of a large organization, you may be able to obtain the help of your group's speaker's bureau. The people staffing these operations arrange, prepare, and promote presentations. Their help can save you hours of work.

Off On Your Own

If you have to handle promotion alone, your best approach may be to start small. A simple but informative invitation or press release may be all you need.

If you need more extensive promotion, adapt ideas you've seen used to promote similar presentations. Magazines such as *Sales Promotion* and *Audio Visual Communications* regularly contain features on techniques used to promote presentations of all types.

One guiding principle to keep in mind if you're preparing your own promotion is this: Never mistake your package for your product. This means you should concentrate your promotional efforts on the benefits you're offering, not on the details of your presentation. Audiences don't attend presentations because they consist of a 20-minute script, 4,000 slides, 20 projectors, all integrated in a multi-image presentation controlled by the new Golly-G programmer. Only hard-core gadgetry and technique "freaks" would be attracted by statistics like that. Instead, people want to know what's in the presentation for ol' Number One. So you must attract them by promising information, or a product, or a candidate, or a startling idea that will change their lives for the better. Will you show them a car that cuts fuel costs dramatically? Give them techniques to sell products more effectively? Teach them strategies to protect their investments? Train them in more efficient ways to assemble a product? Whatever it is that your presentation promises, make sure that promise is highlighted in your promotion.

When you promote your presentation, follow the advice of an old advertising maxim: "Sell the sizzle, not the steak."

Or, to translate it into the language of your preparation: "Promote the audience payoff, not the presentation."

To Build an Audience, You Try and Try Again

What does it take to promote a presentation?

If you're a salesperson trying to interest prospects in seeing a desktop presentation, an appealing direct mail letter (or, better yet, letters) may be all you need.

If you're the promotion chairperson for a trade association seminar or conference, mailings to association members plus "newsy" press releases to association journals and newspapers should build interest in your presentation.

And if you're promoting a presentation for general audiences, you can try just about every appropriate technique in the field of advertising and promotion.

"We can never be absolutely sure what works," says Jennifer Wood, managing director of *The Great Toronto Adventure* and one of the people who has to judge the value of the presentation's promotional efforts. "We try a number of different approaches, and we survey our audiences to find out how they learned about the presentation. But that only tells us what has worked. It doesn't necessarily give us a guide to what will work in the future."

To attract viewers to *The Great Toronto Adventure*, an hour-long multi-image show on Toronto created from more than 4,000 slides and computer-directed visual and sound effects, Wood and her colleagues have used the following:

• Brochures. A half million are distributed every year through hotels, the Toronto airport, tourist information centers located on major highways leading into Canada, tour agencies, the Convention and Tourist Bureau of Metropolitan Toronto, the Ontario Ministry of Industry and Tourism, and all other attractions in the city. In the show's first year, publicity people used a four-page full-color brochure; in the second year, a six-page four-color brochure; and in the third year, a four-page two-color brochure. The longer four-color brochure attracted more people. Or did it? Was it the impact of the brochure that filled the theatre or just the fact that the show was new? As Wood says, you can't be sure. But she and her colleagues are considering a return to a more colorful brochure.

• A two-page full-color ad in the guide to Toronto, published monthly and distributed through hotels and motels.

• Press releases to newspapers, magazines, radio and television stations. This material is distributed on a regular basis, says Wood. Their goal is to keep the presentation in the eyes of editors–and thus, they hope, in the awareness of readers and listeners–by developing new and fresh reasons for visiting the presentation.

• Co-op radio and newspaper advertising. One way visitors get around Toronto is by public transportation (the city's buses and subways have an excellent reputation for on-time, efficient service). To capitalize on this, the show's man-

A variety of promotional materials is used to attract visitors to *The Great Toronto Adventure.*

agers have entered into a co-op advertising program with the local transit authority.

• Promotions with tour companies. By keeping travel agents, tour operators and bus companies aware of the entertainment value of the presentation, Wood says, the show attracts thousands of out-of-town visitors.

• Listings. Descriptive listings of the show are given in all Ontario Ministry of Industry and Tourism publications, Convention and Tourist Bureau of Metropolitan Toronto publications, tour guide books published in and outside of Canada, and all association publications relating to tourism.

How effective are these various approaches? Wood says their audience survey results show that 30 percent of the people who come to see *The Great Toronto Adventure* learn about the presentation from the brochure. Another 30 percent come as a result of the two-page ad in the guide to Toronto. (The appeal of the ad is reinforced by having copies of the brochure available in hotel lobbies.) Fifteen percent of the presentation's visitors learn about it by word of mouth, 8 percent are groups booked through tour operators and travel agents, and 7 percent read the listings in publications of the Ontario Ministry of Industry and Tourism and the Convention and Tourist Bureau of Metropolitan Toronto. Discount coupon programs and other street and special offer promotions each account for about 5 percent of the presentation's viewers.

Obviously, some approaches are more successful than others. But unless you're absolutely certain that a particular promotional piece will work, Wood suggests you try several approaches to reach your audience.

"We even have people on Bloor Street (where the presentation is located) walking around in costume, distributing brochures and balloons," says Wood. "We thought this would be an extremely effective way to attract people who were walking by the theatre. However, being a year-round attraction, we soon learned we were busiest during inclement and very hot weather."

The moral? As any advertising executive will tell you, don't rely on a single approach–be it an ad, press release, or brochure. When it comes to promoting a product or a presentation, success is usually the result of repetition.

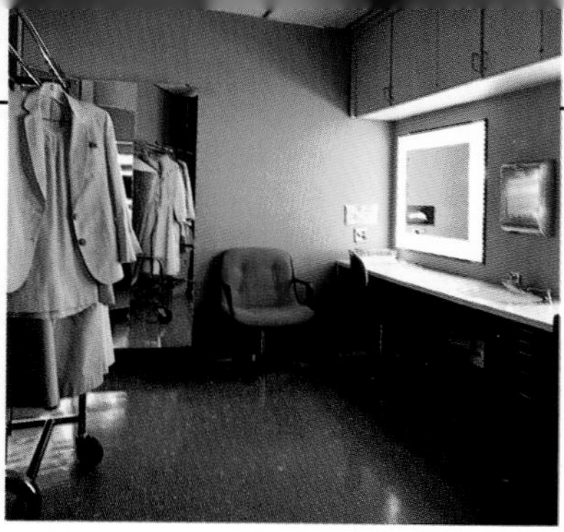

9 Getting Yourself Ready

In the earlier chapters, we wrote about presentations as if they were merely the sums of various eternal factors–script, visuals, projectors, screens. Well, there's one element that's been left out of the formula, the catalyst for all the others. And that element is you.

You are to a presentation what Jane Fonda or Robert Redford are to a movie–the star, the leading character, the focal point around which all the other elements revolve.

You're it.

So now it's time to get *you* ready.

That's right, you're going to work on yourself now. You're going to perform a simple ritual that athletes refer to as "psyching up." You're going to start thinking about your presentation and yourself in such a way that you'll find it difficult to wait to step out in front of your audience. And best of all, you'll know, as you wait to make your presentation, that you'll be a success. Relax: You can almost hear them clapping already.

Getting yourself into this expectant frame of mind involves preparing yourself internally and externally. Your internal "psyching" helps you organize and orchestrate your attitude and your self-confidence. Your external "psyching" helps you polish your appearance. Once completed, these preparations result in a presenter who, to borrow a phrase from show business, is ready "to knock 'em dead."

Wait, you say. This just isn't you. You'll never be able to go before an audience with that kind of confidence and self-assurance. Maybe not. But then again, maybe it's time you tossed aside that negative attitude and self-image and started thinking about yourself in a new way.

It's All In Your Mind

How do you feel about making presentations? Do you look forward to the experience? Enjoy it? Try to find opportunities to make additional presentations? If so, that's great. You probably don't need most of the lessons in this chapter.

As for you others: Do you hate to even think about making presentations? Does the prospect of making one leave you feeling weak? Would you rather schedule open heart surgery than stand before an audience? If so, don't cringe with shame. After all, you have plenty of company. Most people have a negative attitude about making presentations.

But since you're reading this book, the chances are you'd rather leave the ranks of this large second group and join that lucky bunch of people who can stand before an audience at the drop of an invitation.

Well, you can. It's simple.

All you have to do is change your mind.

That's right, the positive or negative feelings you associate with making a presentation are all in your mind. There's nothing inherently positive or negative, frightening or exhilarating, about standing up in front of people and speaking to them. In reality—which can be defined as the situation minus any interpretation you might put on it—making a presentation is merely saying a few hundred words. That means if you find the occasion of a presentation to be anxiety-producing, it's because you put the anxiety in. It's not there to begin with. Just ask the people who enjoy making presentations.

Changing your attitude toward presentations from negative to positive is going to require a little mental housecleaning. You have to throw out all the ideas you've been gathering and storing over the years concerning the difficulties associated with making presentations.

First to go should be the paranoid feeling that your audience is against you. Unless you're addressing a convention of misanthropes, it isn't true. It's far more likely that the people in your audience want you to succeed. (Why else would they have come?) They want to hear your ideas and see your visuals, because they have an interest in your presentation (their motivations, remember?). Some of them may have even paid money or traveled a considerable distance or interrupted a busy schedule to hear you. What better vote of confidence in your abilities could you want?

So think positively: You're the people's choice.

The next piece of mental rubbish to throw out is the feeling that you're incapable of making a presentation. Once again, it's just not true. If you've ever told a joke, you're capable. If you've ever asked for a raise, you're capable. If you've ever told your friends about the dress you almost bought or the fish that got away, you're capable. In other words, unless you're afflicted with an incapacitating handicap, you're capable of getting up in front of a group of people and making a presentation. In fact, you've been making presentations since you learned how to talk. You're making them now, everyday of the week. And chances are you're pretty good at it. You just never gave yourself credit.

So think positively: You have what it takes.

The last bit of scrap we can toss out of your attic of negative attitudes is the feeling that whatever you have to say will sound trite. It seems that just about every presenter, at one time or another, has experienced this emotion. After working on a presentation for weeks or months, the presenter begins to experience doubt. The ideas and words that once sounded so intelligent and exciting now sound banal and flat. The presenter then concludes that he or she doesn't have what it takes to develop a successful presentation.

It's another example of faulty thinking. The fact is that it's the rare presentation that strikes most viewers as completely original. Most presentations, by contrast, consist of commonplace ideas wrapped in new packaging. That packaging might be based on a new twist to an old idea (a marketing program introduced in an imitation of Aesop's Fables). Or it might be a takeoff on a current idea (a presentation of sales techniques explained in the style of the Peter Principle). Or it might be an out-and-out steal of a currently popular idea* (following the success of the movie *Star Wars*, dozens of companies modeled their sales meetings after the film's opening sequence and its tag line, "May the Force be with you!"). So you don't have to be uncommonly clever to make an effective presentation. You just have to be creative enough to package everyday ideas in new ways. If you can do that, you won't have to worry about being trite.

So think positively: Your ideas are sound.

*Make sure that you have the legal approvals necessary whenever you use copyrighted themes, music, etc.

Restructuring Your Attitude

Once you rid your mind of the belief that you're incapable of making interesting presentations, you have to restock it with more positive attitudes–ones that will allow you to stand before your audiences with confidence. Here are some suggestions that can get you started with your attitude restructuring program:

1. See yourself as helpful. You have something extremely valuable to give an audience. That something may be entertainment–a presentation of humorous anecdotes and visuals that leave people with a good feeling. Or that something may be information–facts, figures, details, and explanations of new ideas, plans, proposals, or products. Naturally, if you hold negative attitudes about making presentations, this idea about helping an audience seems like nonsense. But put yourself in your audience's place and consider their motivations. They may need better products or more effective sales programs or improved services. If your presentation tells them how to get what they need, you're doing them a favor. Even if your product or plan isn't the right one for them, that information is still helpful. And that means you're helpful. So see yourself this way.

2. See yourself as prepared. As already discussed in Chapter 7, there's no better way to get yourself in the right frame of mind for a presentation than to rehearse. Confidence and competence come with practice, so don't forget the lesson of that chapter–rehearse, rehearse, rehearse, until you're familiar and comfortable with your material.

3. See yourself as in control. When you're in control, you're confident. You're in charge, the Big Cheese, Numero Uno. You call the shots. Of course, in one sense, that's what this entire book is about–the preparations you must make to assume and maintain control of your presentation. If you know what you want to accomplish, you're in control. If you know how to appeal to your audience's motivations, you're in control. If you know how to write your script, assemble your visuals, and operate your equipment, you're in control. In fact, every decision that you make and every act that you engage in gives you another measure of control. Remember that. Dwell on that. It's the most powerful confidence-builder you can use.

Building the Habit of a Positive Attitude

Yes, it's hard to implement new attitudes into your consciousness just by the power of positive thought. You have to go beyond thinking to action. You have to plan, walk, and talk as if these new attitudes were already a part of your personality.

Here are a few suggestions for creating positive mental habits:

• **Use mental rehearsal.** All your rehearsals don't have to be live, with you in front of your colleagues or a mirror. You can rehearse a dozen times a day, whenever you have free time in fact, by just sitting back in a chair, relaxing, and imagining yourself giving that presentation.

The use of mental rehearsal to build positive habits is an old and effective technique. The reason for its longevity and popularity is that *it works*. As Dr. Arnold Lazarus, professor of psychology at the Graduate School of Applied and Professional Psychology at Rutgers University, writes in his book *In the Mind's Eye*, "If you repeatedly and conscientiously picture yourself achieving a goal, your chances of actual success are greatly enhanced."

Dr. Lazarus has, in fact, used this sort of mental rehearsal to help people who suffer from stage fright. He advises his patients to see themselves on a stage, in front of an audience, performing just as they want to perform. The point of such practice, he states, is not to turn average people into exceptional performers. Instead, he writes, "The deliberate practice of goal rehearsal can maximize and actualize whatever potential talents and abilities lie dormant in a person." In short, if you can imagine yourself making a successful presentation, you probably will.

• **Get experience.** There's no better way to strengthen positive attitudes in yourself than to get experience as a presenter. There are a number of ways you can do this—even if your self-confidence is still a little shaky. One of the easiest and most reassuring ways, as mentioned in the Introduction, is to join an organization such as Toastmasters. Toastmaster groups meet regularly, providing an opportunity for members to speak before a supportive audience.

Another simple way to get experience is to teach. Perhaps you can volunteer your knowledge and expertise to your company's training department. You probably talk to people about your work already—at home, parties, meetings, at the club. So to do it in a classroom or workshop shouldn't raise your anxiety level to the point of discomfort.

If you do feel comfortable in this role, you also might look for opportunities to teach at schools or colleges in your community. Many adult education and continuing education courses are taught by part-time instructors—men and women who use their 9-to-5 experiences as a syllabus for their courses.

• **Learn to relax.** Tension destroys feelings of self-assurance and self-confidence and undermines positive attitudes. It's hard to feel you're in control of a situation, capable of handling whatever comes up, if your body is as rigid as an I-beam. In fact, when you're physically rigid you're also probably mentally rigid. That means your mind won't be adaptable enough to handle the presentation situation as it evolves from moment to moment.

When Something Goes Wrong

Physical relaxation, on the other hand, usually brings mental sharpness and flexibility. A relaxed presenter is alive, animated, forceful, aware of his or her audience, and responsive to its reactions.

This being the case, you're better off making your presentation while relaxed. Getting yourself into the proper state of relaxation—calm, confident, and alert—is a process that's easily learned. Techniques such as Transcendental Meditation or the Relaxation Response can be learned in less than a day. Biofeedback training usually takes a little longer, but the scientific underpinning of the technique often helps convince skeptics of its effectiveness.

One technique that combines not only progressive relaxation but also mental rehearsal is Attention Control Training. It was developed by Dr. Robert Nideffer, a clinical psychologist, who has used it to help athletes, musicians, and others who experience tension and anxiety under the pressure of public performances. A client using Dr. Nideffer's technique first learns to relax the entire body. Then the person is asked to visual-

Presenters—both would-be and polished—have their own chambers of horror. When they enter these rooms—usually in their imaginations but sometimes in actuality—they're usually faced with one or more of the following catastrophes:

As the presentation begins, every visual that appears on the screen is upside down.

Three minutes into the presentation, the projector lamp burns out.

When they turn on the recorded portion of their presentation, all they hear is the flap-flap-flap of broken tape.

Just as they're about to enunciate their major theme, the microphone goes dead, only to come back seconds later with a series of extraterrestrial screeches.

As they begin to state their conclusion. . . .

No more, you say! You don't want to be reminded of what can go wrong. Well, that's not the point. The point is that when these mistakes and malfunctions occur they don't have to be catastrophes. You don't have to approach a presentation as a potential chamber of horrors.

All you have to do is be prepared.

That means that while you don't expect things to go wrong when you step to the podium, you acknowledge that every once in a while something will. And when that happens, you're ready, just like the television announcer whose voice comes on over a blank screen to tell you that "due to technical problems beyond our control we have lost our picture temporarily."

You don't have to use that line, but you should have your own version ready. Then, when something goes wrong, just stop your presentation and calmly tell your audience, "We seem to be having a problem. Let me get everything squared away and we'll get started again." Then go about the business of righting whatever's wrong.

This sort of an approach gives an audience confidence in your professionalism. You'll look and sound like you know what you're doing, so they'll expect you to clear up the problem and resume the presentation.

The opposite approach, to panic and run around helter-skelter trying to patch things up, just leaves an audience feeling that you're a presenter at wit's end. They're likely to lose confidence in you and your message.

So be prepared. Don't expect things to go wrong. But don't panic and lose control when they do. Just tell your audience what's happened and about how long it'll take to clear up the problem. They'll appreciate your straightforwardness, and all but the time-pressed will probably stick with you.

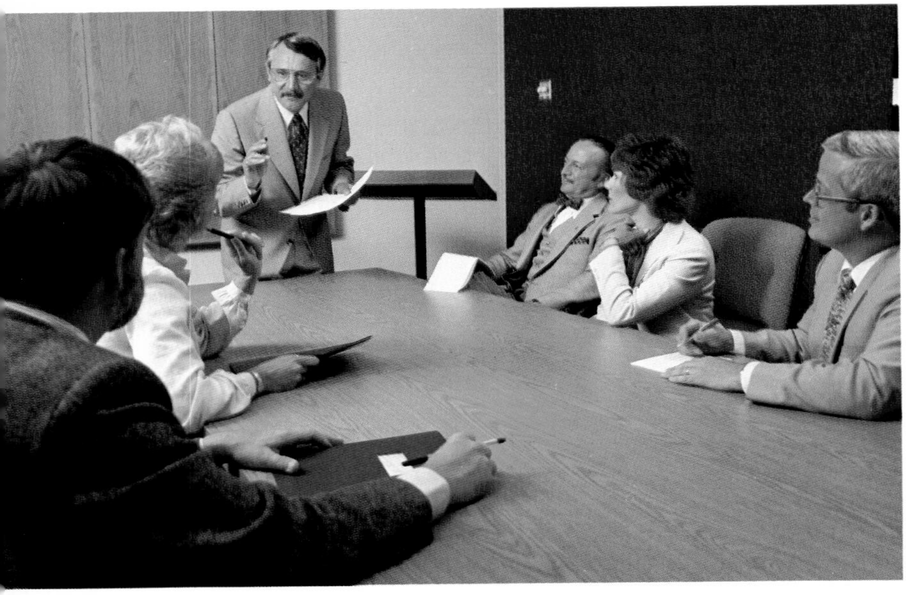

ize two situations. The first involves an experience the client regards as a failure. As feelings of anxiety begin to flood the individual, he or she is instructed to relax, to stop visualizing the anxiety-producing scene, and then to begin visualizing a second scene–a situation in which he or she acts and reacts with complete success. The client is then instructed to follow the same procedure in actual situations. When anxiety starts to build, the client relaxes and refocuses attention on successful behavior.

As Dr. Nideffer writes in his book *Attention Control Training*, "It's the ability to control attention under pressure and in response to changing demands that separates ... the average person from the super-performer."

• **Learn to establish personal contact with an audience.** As mentioned earlier, one reason why people suffer from stage-fright and develop negative attitudes about making presentations is that they see the situation as one of "them vs me." One way you can eliminate that subjective evaluation from your thinking is to see your audience, not as a collection of anonymous faces, but as a gathering of individuals. Thinking along these lines almost forces you to make contact with the people before you. You wouldn't, for example, look at the back of a room or down toward the floor or from side to side if you were talking to a friend. Instead, you'd look right into your friend's eyes to see if your words were getting across.

So do the same thing when speaking before an audience, whether the audience consists of five people or five hundred people. Make eye contact with individual members of the audience.

Look at them as if they were close friends or colleagues. This technique, a form of nonverbal communication, tells your audience two things: One, that you're talking to them, not through them; and two, that you care about them, that you see them as people, not as props. Making contact with your audience and seeing, through their responses, that they're in contact with you, can be an instant builder of confidence.

Another way to establish this sort of rapport with your audience is to speak directly to individual members of the audience. As your eyes move across the room, scanning the eyes of your audience, stop every once in a while and spend a brief period talking directly to one person. This technique, like the one above, communicates to people the feeling that you're talking to them personally. As you gain some experience with presentations, you can try the simple practice of moving toward your audience. Experts who have studied the dynamics of presentations have found that as a presenter lessens the distance between the audience and him or her, the more favorably the audience responds. That, of course, is why professional performers—singers, comedians, the hosts of television talk shows—walk around a stage, moving closer to one section of the audience then another, sometimes even walking directly into the audience. In a very subtle way, it establishes a closer bond between performer and audience, thus increasing the performer's likelihood of success.

Above all else, when you stand before an audience, act natural. Assume a relaxed posture, use gestures that are natural for you, and speak at an unhurried pace. In short, just be yourself. It's wise, of course, to add gestures and movement to your presentation style, but until these gestures and movements come easily, practice them at home or during casual conversations with friends. Don't make the mistake of walking out in front of an audience like a first-year debater, instructed in the importance of gestures but unskilled in their use. The effect created is puppet-like and humorous—and almost certain to distract from your message.

A Manner of Speaking

Put an inexperienced presenter before an audience and he or she is likely to behave as if a bomb were ticking in the podium. Words pour forth in a torrent, sentences run one into the next, and the emphasis of rhythm and intonation are swept away in a breathless rush to the last sentence of the presentation. When the presentation is over, you can almost hear the presenter inhale a great gulp of air and then expel it with a prolonged sigh.

The effect of such a sprint-like performance leaves an audience speechless—at a loss for words because they're not quite sure what the speaker said. Audiences need time to digest and assimilate a speaker's words *and* thoughts; unlike reading, listening doesn't allow the person on the receiving end of the message the luxury of review.

So when you speak, consider your listeners. Do everything you can to make it easy for them to hear and comprehend you. Any one of a number of books on speech-making can help you develop an effective speaking voice and style.

Until you can read these books, at least develop the three following suggestions:

1. Try to sound calm and confident. Rapid speech is a classic sign of anxiety, and if an audience detects anxiety in your voice, they're bound to be distracted and uncomfortable. So speak in a relaxed manner.

2. Speak at a pace that allows an audience to comprehend your ideas. As mentioned above, it's not enough for the audience just to hear your words. They have to keep track of those words, build them into ideas, then build the ideas into the logic of your message. To do this they need time to think as well as listen. You can give them that time by talking at a rate of about 125 words a minute. To get a feel for that pace, mark off a 125-word section in this or another book, then read it aloud as you time yourself. Try it several times, until you're completing the passage just as the second hand of your watch or clock passes the 60-second mark.

3. Don't garble your words. Marlon Brando may have become a star by playing characters who mumbled. You probably won't. You must carefully enunciate your words if you are to sound intelligent and informed. If mumbling or slurring or shortening words are part of your current speech habits, you may have to play Henry Higgins to yourself.

How to Dress Up Your Performance

Do clothes make the man or woman? More specifically, do clothes influence an audience's reaction to a speaker?

Our nation's egalitarian spirit says "no." Clothes don't matter. Ideas, intelligence, personality–these are the factors that count.

But John T. Molloy begs to differ. Molloy is a former teacher, who, on a part-time job, began studying the influence of a teacher's clothing on classroom effectiveness. What he discovered fascinated him: Clothes *did* make a difference, a significant difference.

Molloy quit his job as a teacher, expanded his studies, computerized the results, and became a much-sought-after consultant on the effects of clothing. After he wrote his first book, *Dress for Success*, *Time* magazine called him "America's first wardrobe engineer." Since then he has written a second book on the importance of clothing, *The Woman's Dress for Success Book*.

The thrust of these books, in Molloy's words, is "always use clothing as a tool." In other words, select your clothes to help you reach your goals. One way a presenter can do this is to go back to his or her analysis of audience motivations. This information defines what an audience wants to hear. The next question is: "From what sort of a person would they most likely accept the answer?" Are they more likely to accept a person who projects an image of "prestige?" Or "honesty?" Or "leadership?" Or maybe an audience would grant more acceptance to someone whose image was that of a "trusting nextdoor neighbor." Whatever answer the presenter arrives at, he or she must dress to fit that part.

If you need help in this area, we suggest you start with Molloy's books. In them you'll find information and tips on selecting everything from shirts to shoes. If you don't have time to read the books before your next presentation, you might find it useful to follow several of Molloy's more general rules:

• Always look clean and neat. Quite simply, if you're going to sound like an expert, then look like an expert. Admittedly, no one's quite sure what an expert looks like, but most people would picture him or her as fresh-scrubbed and wrinkle-free. Whatever you do, don't show up for your presentation in a rumpled suit and a stained tie. That says "sloppiness," and according to Molloy's studies, it's enough to turn off an audience.

• Dress as well as the people in your audience. The reason: You can lose an audience by looking either too superior or too inferior to them. People are more likely to listen to someone from the same social, educational, and economic level as they, and clothing is frequently used as an indicator of these levels.

• If you're unsure of the type of audience you'll find, dress more conservatively than normal. A conservatively dressed person can be accepted by a casually dressed audience, but a speaker in a Hawaiian-print sports shirt would find it hard to get the attention and interest of a suit-and-vest audience.

For a presenter, the right attire is often as important as a forceful script and visuals.

• **Always look as if you're in control.** If you're in front of an audience, it's because the people in that audience consider you an authority on something. So look the part. Project an image of authority. For men, that might mean wearing a suit (but remember, the occasion will determine if suit and tie are the correct image of authority). For women, that could mean wearing a dress or a skirted suit.

In addition to his more general dress rules, Molloy has established several rules that apply particularly to presenters.

• **Create contrast between face and clothes.** Don't evaluate your wardrobe solely on what it looks like in your bedroom mirror. Consider what you're going to look like to a person sitting in the rear of the presentation room. Your cream-colored suit, shirt, and tie might appear striking as you admire yourself at home, but you might look like the Pillsbury Doughboy to people in the last row of seats. Your best approach, suggests Molloy, is to create a crisp definition of form. Use a high-contrast combination of clothes, such as a dark blue suit or dress, with a white shirt, and for men, a dark blue tie.

• **Don't blend into the background.** If the stage you're appearing on is draped with a dark blue curtain, you're going to appear lost if you wear a dark blue suit. So once again, wear something that establishes contrast between you and the background.

• **Avoid odd patterns.** If you want to lose your audience in a hurry, come to your presentation dressed as a carnival barker.

Television producers suggest several other guidelines for dress for that medium:

• **Dress to compensate for the technical limitations of the medium.** To a color video camera, your clothing represents information it must process. In most cases, this information is handled without technical difficulty. But there are certain colors and patterns which, if they dominate the image area, will cause distortion in picture quality.

The two colors to avoid, say the experts, are red and white. Too much red in your wardrobe—say a turtleneck sweater without a jacket, or an all-red dress—will cause the video cameras to begin "bleeding" color from the garment into other areas of the picture. Too much stark white in your wardrobe will cause facial tones to go dark.

Pronounced patterns such as houndstooth checks or wide stripes cause what television technicians call a moiré effect, the continuous, undulating movement of what in reality are solid lines. For viewers at home, the effect is that of watching someone with an electric jacket or dress.

The point of a television presentation should be to focus attention on you and your ideas or opinions. So select clothing that doesn't compete with you for attention.

• **Keep your clothing simple.** This point is further amplification of the preceding one. The styling of your clothes and the combinations you wear can also distract viewers from your message. Viewers watching a man or woman dressed in avant-garde fashions will find their attention drawn to—and possibly repelled by—the subject's clothing. The same is true in situations where the person on the screen is wearing inappropriate combinations of clothing, such as a sports coat over an imprinted T-shirt. Of course, there are times when unusual styles and combinations are appropriate. If, for instance, the person wearing avant-garde fashions were the proprietor of a trend-setting clothing boutique, that clothing might be perfect for the occasion.

Most people, however, want to convey an image of stability and sobriety, and for this purpose a more conservative selection of clothes is appropriate. For men, that selection might include a shirt, tie, and suit coat of solid colors (earth tones are best) or subtle patterns. It also could include a turtleneck sweater worn under a sports coat.

For women, the choice of clothing is a little wider. A suit, a dress, a blazer and blouse, a sweater, or a blouse and sweater combination are all appropriate. The question of pants or skirt can be answered by watching the show on which you plan to appear. Some shows stick to medium shots and close-ups, which means the subject on camera is never shown below the waist. Other shows use longer shots, meaning a guest can expect her full wardrobe, including shoes, to be seen. In shows such as these, many producers prefer women to wear a skirt. But that's only because women's fashions, at least as of this writing, regard the skirt as the more acceptable "business" attire.

When selecting an outfit to wear on television, keep one additional thought in mind: The studio sound technicians will need a place to clip on a microphone. A turtleneck sweater, worn without a jacket, doesn't supply the openings or folds needed for the clip. For the same reason, women shouldn't wear long necklaces. They may interfere with the placement of the microphone.

• **Don't detract from your face.** When a television camera zooms in for a head and shoulders close-up of a subject, it creates, in effect, a frame. Everything within that frame competes for attention; everything outside that frame, at least for the moment, doesn't exist. Keep this fact in mind when selecting the clothing and accessories for your television appearance. Large, shiny or unusual earrings, for example, call attention to themselves. A blouse with a large frilly collar or a collar with a large bow will be exaggerated in close-ups and thus call attention to the clothing. Too much make-up diverts attention. An unusual choker necklace attracts attention to itself. And every time attention is attracted away from your face, chances are it's also attracted away from your message.

When appearing on television, wear clothing that focuses attention on your face.

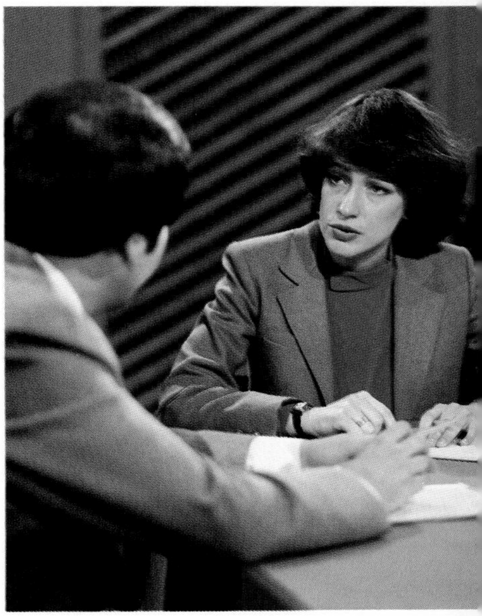

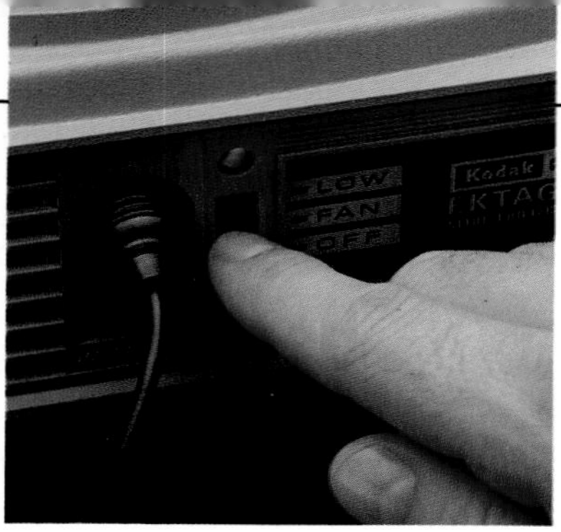

10 The Wrap-up

It's over.

Your presentation is history. The audience is applauding and the lights are going up. Now, are you ready for what comes next?

Next?

Yes, there's more. In the vast majority of presentations, the presenter just doesn't bask in an audience's acceptance and approval, then turn and walk away. If the presentation has been interesting and effective, the audience is going to have some questions. So it's time for you to play the expert.

Are you prepared?

That's right–just as you prepared your script and visuals, you must prepare to answer your audience's questions. But don't look alarmed; you don't have to block out more large chunks of time on your calendar. This preparation is actually an extension of the preparations you made for your formal presentation. Only now what you must do is anticipate questions your audience might raise as a result of what you say. Then you must mentally prepare suitable answers.

Most likely, the questions will be of several basic types; questions concerning the basic content of your presentation–the how-do-you-know-that type of question; questions asking for clarification or expansion of certain points in your presentation–the tell-me-more type question; questions asking you to assess the implications of your conclusions–the what-does-it-all-mean type of question; questions asking you to focus on viewpoints counter to your own–the that's-not-what-I-read-somewhere type of question; and finally, questions that challenge the entire thesis and development of your presentation–the you're-so-far-off-base-that-I-just-had-to-say-something type of question.

Some of these questions could throw an unprepared presenter. But if you're ready–if you've anticipated the questions, prepared answers, and mentally rehearsed the delivery of these answers–you're less likely to lose your balance. Like an expert, you can maintain control of the session.

The anticipation of questions and the preparation of rehearsed answers might sound like an attempt at deception. After all, question and answer periods are supposed to be spontaneous, an

You rarely say it all, so allow time for questions following your formal presentation.

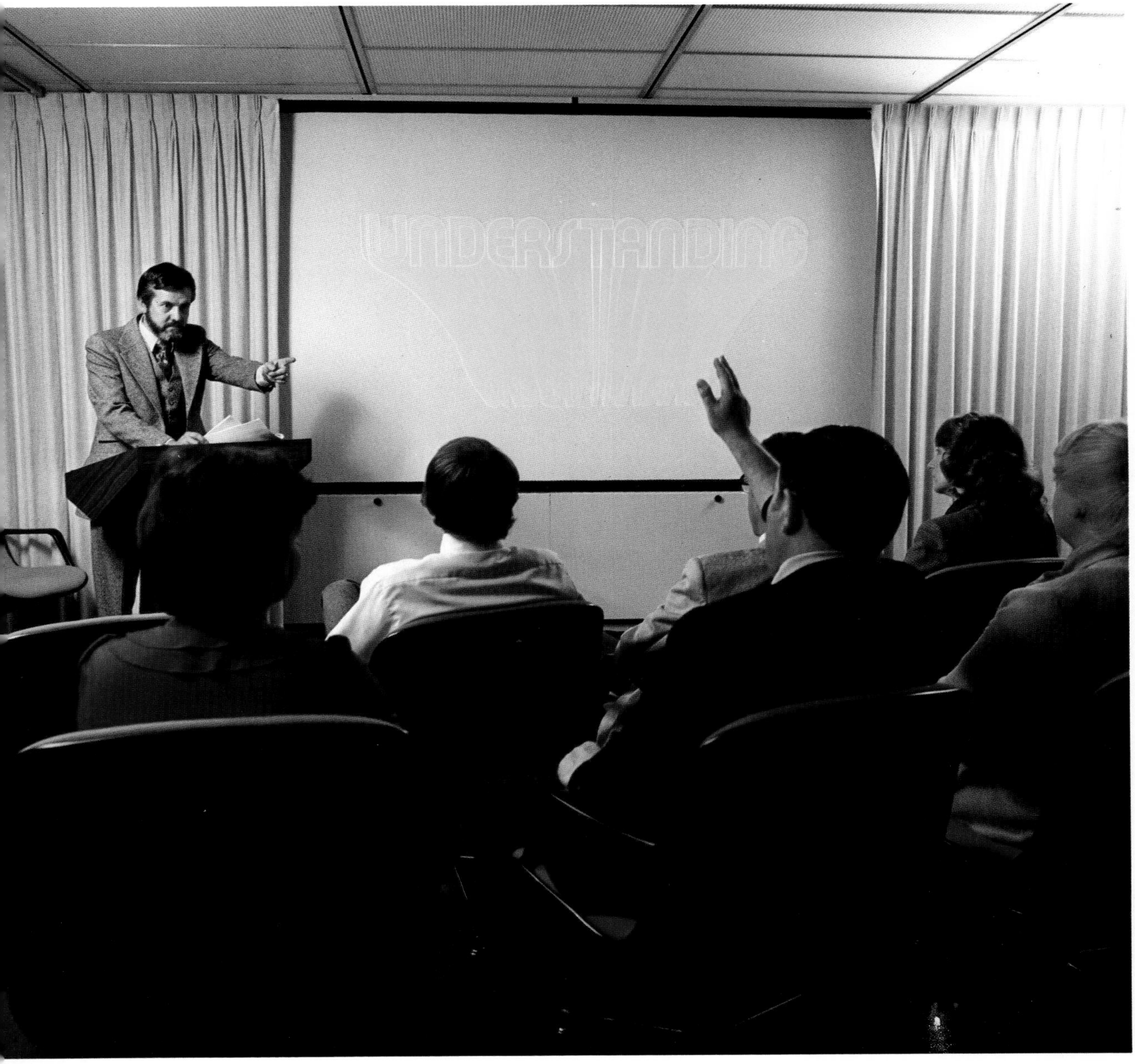

unrehearsed conversation between speaker and audience. And sometimes that's all they are. If, for example, your presentation is little more than the quilting together of anecdotes from the field of sports, you don't have to prepare extensively for questions. For the most part, people will just want to hear more of the same. But if you're a sales rep demonstrating a product, or a financial manager making a presentation, you'll want to be thoroughly prepared for the tough questions you can expect. Of course, your answers can sound spontaneous—and probably should. But behind that spontaneity should be thorough and thoughtful preparation.

This, by the way, has been the approach taken by a number of U.S. presidents prior to major press conferences. The president has key members of his staff compile a list of probable questions—and acceptable answers. The president then reads the questions and memorizes the essence of the answers. He follows this, when appropriate, with a rehearsal, with his staff members playing the role of reporters. It's because of this preparation that a president usually appears well-informed and certain of his answers. Facts, figures, details—all are on the tip of his tongue.

A president puts this much effort into preparation because he wants to project an image of competence and confidence. For exactly the same reason, you should take an identical approach.

Fielding the Questions

If you prepare yourself properly, you shouldn't have difficulty answering most of the questions asked of you. Give your answer in a straightforward manner, trying to remain brief but informative. Also, if a number of people are vying for your attention, make sure you take questions from different parts of the room.

That's the easy part. The hard part comes when someone asks a difficult question—difficult not because it requires a detailed reply, but because it challenges the very heart of your argument. This sort of question can lock you in a debate—something you want to avoid. Instead, you should aim to state your point, quiet your questioner, and close off any further discussion of the point.

Professional speakers use a number of techniques to handle—or deflect—questions of this kind. Here are some of the more effective:

1. Rephrase the question. This tactic gives you an opportunity to turn the question into one for which you have a prepared answer. When you repeat the question (you should always repeat questions for the benefit of audience members who have not heard them), rephrase it in such a way that it allows you to make a point that strengthens your position. Observe a political press conference—any political press conference—and you'll see politicians using this tactic. A reporter's question becomes a springboard for a prepared answer.

2. Agree and disagree. This tactic could be renamed "yes, but." To use it, you agree in general with some part of the question, but then you go on to disagree, in detail, with the main thrust of the question. Example: "Yes, there's some truth in what you've said, but I think such-and-such is closer to the truth because of these reasons." The effect of this tactic is to give the questioner his or her due, then to pull the rug out from under his or her position.

3. Answer a question with a question. Use this tactic when you think a questioner has raised a false issue, one that hides an underlying question or motive. For example, suppose a questioner were to ask, "Do you really believe that electric cars are the answer to the nation's energy crisis?" Let's assume that by the tone of the questioner's voice, you determine the question is meant not to seek information, but to ridicule your position or to set you up for a damaging cross-examination. In such cases, reply with a question: "Before I answer that, let me ask you why you think electric cars aren't a feasible solution?" This forces the questioner to reveal more information on his or her position, giving you the opportunity to dismiss the original question or to expose weak reasoning in the questioner's logic.

4. Ignore the question. Sometime, somewhere, someone will ask you what can only be called a foolish question. To answer it would waste your time and the time of others in the audience.

Questioning the Value of Questions

Is a question-and-answer period necessary in every presentation?

"No," says Andy McKay, a longtime toastmaster from the Rochester, New York area.

"To decide whether a question-and-answer period is necessary or advisable," he says, "just ask yourself one question: Will the session influence the audience? If it won't, then forget about it and put all of your effort into your presentation. But if the probable questions and your answers will influence the audience, then by all means make the session a part of your presentation."

If you do plan on fielding questions from your audience, McKay advises that you be sure the Q-and-A session comes immediately after your presentation. "Don't break for 10 minutes, then expect your audience to come back and ask meaningful questions. It usually won't happen. Their involvement and focus will be broken and you'll wind up staring out into a room of blank faces."

Not only is such a lack of response embarrassing, it also detracts from your overall presentation. The lack of questions gives the impression that no one in the audience took your presentation seriously.

When you do answer questions, McKay offers two important rules: Be honest. And be brief.

"If you have an answer to a question, give it candidly and concisely. If you don't have an answer, say so. If the question is important enough, offer to get an answer to the questioner at a later time or refer the question to someone in the room who could and would be willing to answer." McKay adds, "Don't put someone on the spot, though."

For the most part, adds McKay, Q-and-A sessions are no problem if you do your homework. "The secret," he says, "is to be prepared."

Worse, any answer you give could be seen as an attempt to make the questioner look more foolish. The best way out of such a situation is to simply laugh it off and move on. Be tactful and courteous in doing this, however, lest you appear too haughty. A simple phrase such as, "That's one for the experts in Washington (or at headquarters or at a think tank)," allows you to avoid the question and move on.

5. Admit you're stumped. There may be times when you get a truly tough question, one that goes beyond your level or field of expertise. When that happens be human and admit you don't know the answer. Acknowledge the intelligence and validity of the question, then say something such as, "I wish I could answer that question, but it deals with an area I'm not totally familiar with, so any answer I might give would be superficial at best and misleading at worst." Having said that, you can offer to get a full answer to the question, which you would send to the questioner. This tactic, by the way, is one that sales reps should use if they're making a presentation to people with complex technical questions. Better to say you'll get an answer from an engineer at headquarters than to try to fake a reply.

6. Refuse to answer. The occasions are rare when a questioner will ask for information that you can't or don't want to share, whether it's proprietary or confidential or personal or because it's totally irrelevant to your current presentation. But when a situation such as this comes up, flatly refuse to answer the question. If you can give a reason for your refusal—such as when dealing with proprietary information—offer it. It will make your refusal seem less brusque. Otherwise just say matter of factly that you don't wish to answer the question.

Dealing With Hecklers

Hecklers are a professional hazard for comedians, singers, and politicians, but for most people making presentations they're few and far between.

So don't worry about having to deal with a heckler in your audience. You don't have to prepare a string of Don Rickles put-downs. You should, however, learn to distinguish between a heckler and a persistent but sincere questioner. The difference between the two is quite simple. A heckler just wants attention. He or she wants the people in the audience—and perhaps you—to acknowledge that he or she is intelligent, witty, perceptive, humorous, and far more capable than you. The persistent questioner, on the other hand, wants information. This person wants to know why you feel or think a certain way, how you arrived at a certain conclusion, what assumptions you may have made in developing your line of reasoning. This sort of person deserves your attention and your answer; if you can't answer, he or she should get a courteous explanation for your refusal.

But what about that rare occasion when a determined heckler decides he or she needs attention? How should you react?

Experienced presenters offer four suggestions:

1. Ignore the person. This is the best approach to take if you can. The reason: If attention is withheld from a person who's seeking it, there's no psychological reward for his or her behavior, so the behavior is more likely to stop. This approach, of course, demands patience on your part. It's like trying to ignore an itch in the hope that it'll go away. Sometimes it works, sometimes it doesn't.

2. Be polite. When ignoring a heckler won't stop him or her, you have to call on even more of your reserves of patience and be polite to the heckler. You can do this if you just remember the person's motivation: He or she probably feels inadequate in your presence and is trying to compensate for this painful emotion by diverting attention from you. Your approach in this situation should be to allow the heckler a few seconds of limelight, then politely thank him or her for the contribution and move on.

3. Use humor. If you can think of a humorous or witty reply to a heckler, use it. But make sure your remark is witty, not a stage comedian's crude put-down. Calling your heckler "a valid justification for mercy killing" might get a few laughs from your audience, but it's also almost certain to further antagonize your unwanted guest.

Genuine humor, on the other hand, usually can win over your audience and silence a heckler. It was just this sort of approach that Frederick R. Kappel, then chairman and chief executive officer of AT&T, used at a shareholder meeting to silence a heckler and diffuse the tension that had built up in the audience. Four thousand people were in attendance and the meeting had run beyond its scheduled ending. At this point a heckler began questioning Kappel on the company's contributions. It became obvious he was seeking attention, not information. At one point he asked how much the company had given to charities.

"Ten million dollars last year," answered Kappel.

At that the heckler yelled back, "I think I'm going to faint."

"That," replied Kappel, "would be very helpful."

Kappel's witty remark stirred the audience to laughter, quieting the heckler and restoring calm to the meeting. If you're going to be that effective, however, you have to know what you're doing. If you have a gift for effective repartee, by all means use it. If not, you're better off relying on one of the other tactics.

4. Never lose your temper. If you let your temper get the best of you, the heckler has gained the upper hand. Most hecklers love nothing more than to get into a shouting match with a presenter. That gives them all the attention they desire. It also detracts from the personal image the presenter has worked hard to create during his or her presentation. So never lose your temper; it only invites disaster.

11 On The Road

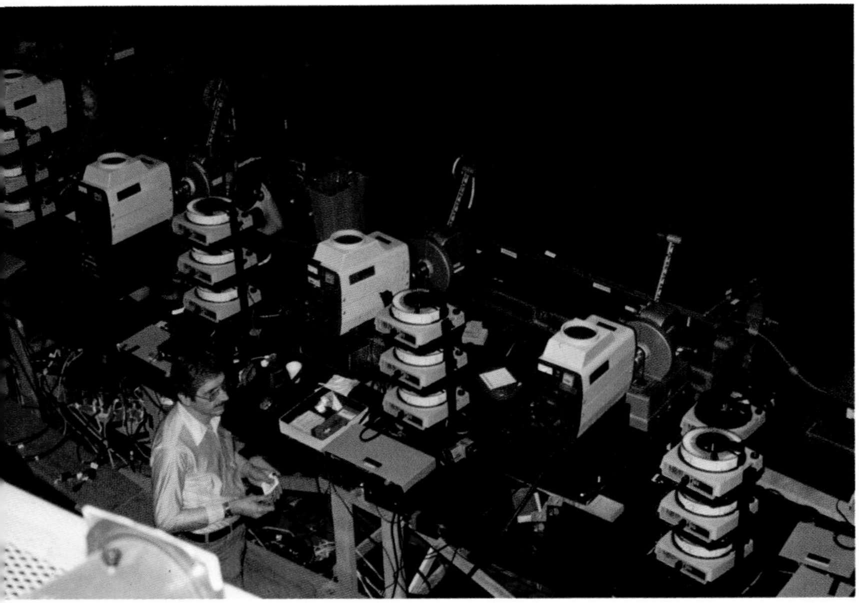

It's a situation that's been repeated countless times:

Al, a marketing manager, has been asked to make a presentation 200 miles from his home office. He arrives, sets up his equipment, runs through his presentation once. Everything works according to plan. He relaxes.

Then, as his audience begins to arrive, he switches on his slide projectors again. Only this time one doesn't light up. A lamp has burned out. And Al doesn't have a spare. So he does the only thing left to do. He becomes frantic.

He rushes to the person who set up the meeting. Does he have a spare lamp? No. How about a local AV dealership? It probably does, but it's a 30-minute drive round trip. There's no way Al can postpone the beginning of the presentation, so he steps before his audience and sheepishly explains that he had brought along some slides, but....

That's a situation you want to avoid. Even if your personality is as resilient as a rubber duck, your enthusiasm drains away while you explain why you're ad-libbing your presentation. Of course, your audience understands; most people are sympathetic. But no matter how kind and considerate an audience you face, and no matter how effective you are without the missing element of your presentation, the fact is an important part of your message won't be seen or heard by your audience. And that hurts.

Of course, this sort of situation wouldn't be worth mentioning if it didn't happen so often. It's not that presenters are unusually absent-minded or overanxious; it's just that when you consider the rough handling that equipment and materials sometimes get when a presentation goes on the road, it's not surprising that things go wrong. As Murphy has warned us: If something can go wrong, it will–and at the worst possible time.

Preparations for road-bound presentations should take this possibility into consideration. That means you have to follow the advice of the Boy Scouts and be prepared. A burned-out lamp is just a minor inconvenience when you're in your office and a fresh lamp sits on a shelf in your company's storeroom. But when you're 2, 20, or 200 miles away from your office, be sure you have that spare lamp with you.

The amount of preparation you must undertake depends, in large part, on the type of presentation you're giving. If your presentation requires only a small amount of equipment–one or two projectors or a tabletop unit–your preparations may consist of little more than making room in the trunk of your car for equipment, slides, and a few tools and spare parts.

But if you're giving a major presentation–a multimedia or multi-image production–your logistical problems can be considerable. You can, however, make these preparations easier if you tackle them according to a systematic plan.

Developing a Plan

1. Decide what equipment and supplies you'll need. Make a list that includes not only the equipment you'll actually use for the presentation, but also spare parts, supplies, tools, and other odds and ends you may need to set up or repair your basic equipment. Here are some suggestions:

- Spare equipment. Always take along an extra slide projector. If one of your presentation units malfunctions, you can simply switch units and be ready to go again.

The same is true of dissolve units. Keep an extra one handy just in case your presentation unit fails.

Bringing an extra motion picture projector or multi-image programmer can be a problem. These units are large and heavy and can add considerably to your packing chores and transportation costs. Your best insurance in situations where you would like backup equipment of this sort is to work through a rental agency.

• Slides, tape, and other software. Slides, audiotape, and programming can be lost or destroyed easily. So don't take a chance. Carry an extra set of each. Some presenters feel more secure when they pack one set with their equipment and carry the extra set with them in an attaché case.

• Spare parts. Take along extra projector lamps, fuses, and power cords if you're using slide projectors. If you have the room, pack an extra slide tray. If you're using motion picture projectors, bring an extra take-up reel, as well as additional projection lamps and fuses.

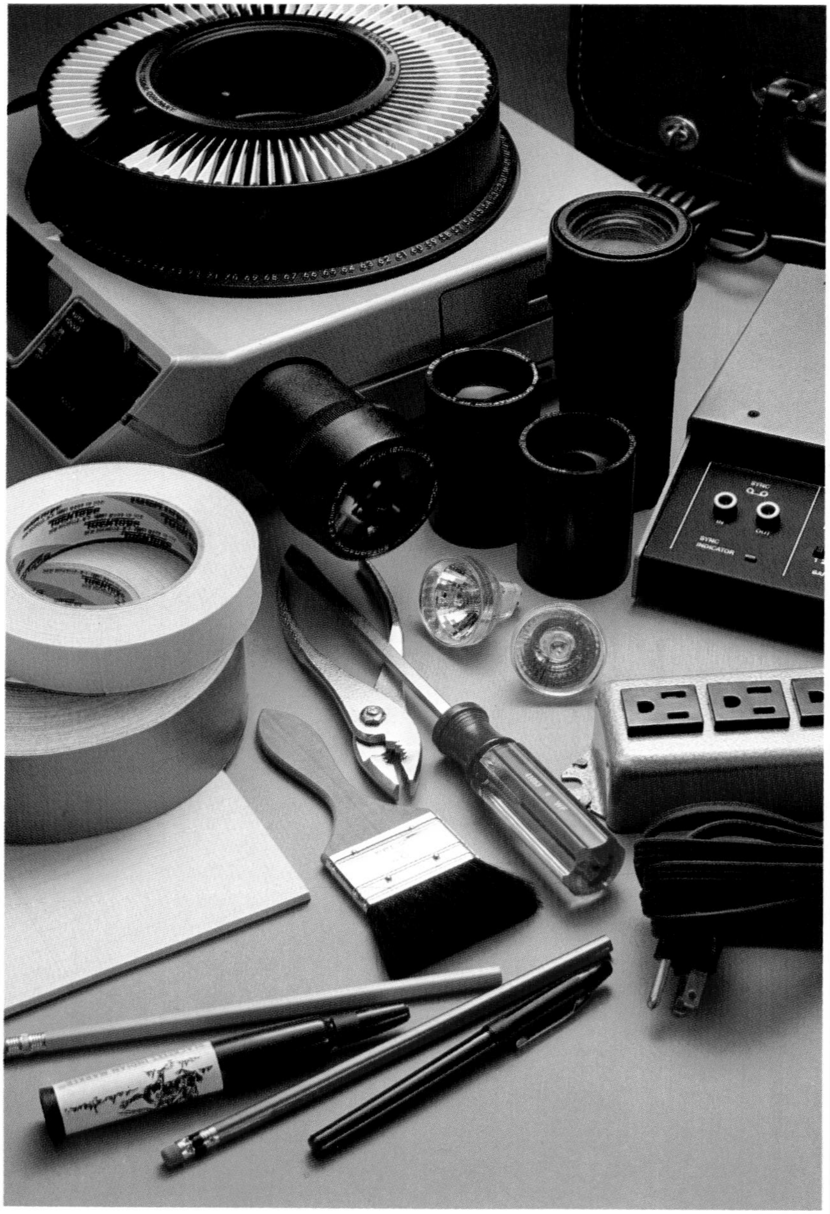

• Tools and supplies. You could fill a page with items that could be included in this category. In fact, people who make presentations on a regular basis, especially major presentations involving a large amount of equipment, usually travel with a tool box filled with everything from screwdrivers to soldering irons and electrical tape. For more modest presentations, however, a set of screwdrivers, nut drivers, and a pair of standard pliers should be sufficient to handle most emergencies. A roll of masking tape and audio splicing tape might also prove helpful. Another common item that you might need now and then is a 3-prong to 2-prong electrical adapter.

2. In certain circumstances, consider using rental services. As mentioned briefly above, there are times when you should consider renting equipment rather than transporting your own. One occasion involves the transportation of large or awkward pieces of equipment, such as the large screens used in multi-image presentations. Since these screens are somewhat fragile and susceptible to marring and scuffing, you're usually better off renting them from audiovisual supply houses that specialize in this service. In almost all cases, these rental houses will ship and erect the screen for you, saving you the time needed for this operation.

Another occasion when renting makes sense is when you need specialized equipment. If, for example, your presentation requires the use of a 35 mm motion picture projector, rent it from a company that will ship it to your presentation site. Try to find a rental agency that can also supply an operator; the more specialized the equipment you rent, the less likelihood that you or your assistants will be able to operate it.

Consider renting microphones, amplifiers, speakers, and other elements of a public address system. Most of this equipment, especially the amplifier and speakers, should be matched to the acoustical requirements of the presentation room. That means with every presentation you make, you could require equipment with different capacities. This consideration alone makes renting the only practical solution.

Look into the economic feasibility of renting equipment if your presentation will be made on a continuing basis, at widely separated locations. Here you must balance the cost of renting versus the cost of transporting your equipment. Sometimes renting can be less expensive. But there's a negative side to renting all of your equipment: You'll always be working with unfamiliar equipment, which, as mentioned in Chapter 7, can lead to problems. But if the rental companies are located in the communities where you'll make your presentations, and if they're willing to supply qualified technicians at the time of your presentations, you may be able to overlook this drawback.

Finally, if your travel budget is limited, consider contracting for presentation services for out-of-town performances. Many audiovisual rental agencies can supply specialists in sound systems, slide and multi-image projection, motion picture projection, and lighting. If your presentation requires any of these services—and you don't have a travel budget for assistants—check the Yellow Pages of the telephone book for the community you'll be visiting. Look under Audiovisual Dealers and Services. The help you need may be a phone call away.

Rugged shipping cases are expensive, but provide protection for equipment transported to presentation sites.

3. Pack your equipment, media, and supplies in rugged shipping cases. It's always with a certain sense of trepidation that a presenter turns over shipping cases to a transporter. They all promise safe and secure delivery. But they also ask if you're interested in insurance.

Buy the insurance. But also take some precautions of your own. And the best precaution you can take is to buy or build shipping cases that are tough and durable enough to survive rough handling. A number of manufacturers sell shipping cases built especially to hold audiovisual equipment. Most of these cases are divided into compartments for projectors, trays, power cords, spare lamps, and parts. In some models, the compartments are lined with foam padding to absorb shocks generated by the impact of bumps and bounces. Yes, this type of shipping case can be expensive. But the equipment you want to protect is also expensive. And then there's the time and money that went into your presentation. Without equipment to give your presentation, that investment loses much of its value. Considered in this light, a rugged shipping case may be worth every penny of its price.

Protective coverings also are available for many desk-top projectors. They too are a worthwhile investment if you plan to use such a unit for traveling presentations.

4. Make shipping and receiving arrangements well ahead of time. This is an aspect of preparation sometimes overlooked by inexperienced presenters. A few days before they're ready to leave with their presentation, they realize they haven't made plans for shipping their equipment. So they rush to a phone book, call an airline or trucking company, and say they have 200 pounds of equipment they'd like delivered to a hotel ballroom 400 miles away by noon the next day. Shortly after that they usually can be heard complaining about the lack of consideration and courtesy shown by people in the transportation industry.

What they should be complaining about, of course, is their own lack of foresight. Moving shipping cases of equipment is not the same as dropping a first-class letter in a mailbox. It's an activity that has to be planned for well in advance of the shipping date. And depending on the number of cases to be shipped and their weight, it may also be an activity that requires the assistance of someone with experience in distribution procedures.

If you will have a lot of equipment to ship, find an expert in shipping procedures. This expert might be someone in your organization's shipping or distribution department, or it might be an agent from one of the companies listed in the Yellow Pages under "Freight Forwarding."

And just as you must arrange to ship your equipment, you must also arrange for someone to receive and store it. If you don't, you could arrive at the presentation site only to find your cases of valuable equipment sitting unprotected on a loading dock. The first person to call to arrange for receiving and storage is the facilities manager at the site of your presentation. Tell him or her when you expect your equipment to arrive and stress that it must be stored in a secure area. If the building can't provide this security, you can probably arrange for your equipment to be received and stored by a local storage company. If this is the case, ask your shipping specialist to help arrange the details. And remember, you not only want the equipment stored, you also want it transported from the storage site to the presentation site. Some freight forwarding companies may provide this temporary storage as part of their regular service. If not, you may have to hire the services of a commercial storage company. You can find them listed under that heading in a telephone book Yellow Pages.

One last reminder: Whether a specialist helps you or whether you handle the shipping arrangements yourself, be sure to insure your equipment. This won't guarantee damage-free delivery, but it spares you replacement bills should equipment be lost or destroyed during shipment. The process of insuring is considerably easier and less time-consuming if you make a complete list of all the equipment you plan to ship. (If the equipment will be shipped in more than one case, make a separate list for each case.) Make copies of these lists, keep one in your files and take another copy with you. If a shipping case should be lost or delayed, you can refer to the list to rent the equipment you'll need.

2 The Presentation Room

We should get one fact straight right at the beginning of this chapter: You don't need a presentation room to produce or give presentations.

People have produced–and continue to produce–outstanding presentations working in offices, conference rooms, storage rooms, and basements. In other words, the lack of a presentation room isn't an excuse for a poorly produced or executed presentation, nor is the availability of one a guarantee of success.

But this doesn't mean that a presentation room is a mere luxury, a gadget-equipped status symbol for the well-heeled organization. A presentation room does serve a definite purpose. If designed properly, a presentation room is a time-saving and labor-saving facility. It serves a presenter the same way a well-organized and equipped workshop serves a cabinetmaker.

The key to designing this kind of presentation workshop is, as the sentence above suggests, thoughtful organization and carefully selected equipment. The room should be laid out with the idea of visual communication in mind. That means the screen area, the projection equipment, and the projection room are the central elements around which the rest of the area should be organized. So as you analyze the central components of your proposed room, ask yourself: What kind of visual support will you use in most of your presentations? How will that material be presented? How will the narrative be delivered? And what kind of communication will the presenter have with the audience? Will the audience participate, simply give feedback, or be part of a "hands-on" activity? All of these are important questions you must answer when you begin the design of a presentation room. And on the basis of your answers, you should begin to put the other elements in place.

The answers to these questions will, of course, also indicate where you should focus in selecting equipment. As in all good purchasing, you should spend your money on your priorities. If, for example, most of your efforts will be focused on three-projector dis-

solve presentations using a live narrator, you should buy the best projectors and dissolve unit you can afford. Similarly, you should buy the best microphone, amplifier, and loudspeakers you can afford. Keep in mind, though, that the best doesn't necessarily mean the most expensive, or even the equipment with the most features. A simple, uncomplicated dissolve control may be best for your needs. It all depends on who uses the equipment and what types of programs will be presented.

If, on the other hand, you find that most of your presentations involve multimedia, multi-image production, you will have to adjust your priorities–and your buying–accordingly. You will need more equipment and more types of equipment. And, naturally, your presentation room will have to be designed to allow you to use and store all the equipment.

Because of the many factors that have to be considered, decisions on how to design a presentation room should be approached deliberately and systematically.

A presentation room need not be elaborate to be efficient and comfortable.

One of the best ways to keep your decision-making deliberate and systematic is to use a checklist that forces you to concentrate on the many elements you'll have to consider.

The following questionnaire and checklist is based on studies made by people at Eastman Kodak Company. It was developed to help them evaluate the needs of the many Kodak organizations wanting to build presentation rooms. With the questions, the group could accurately assess the needs of, for example, a sales group that planned to give presentations to small groups, using materials acquired from a headquarters-based production unit. In the same way they could distinguish these needs from those of a group that needed a presentation room to develop and give training programs. They could also distinguish between the needs of a group that trained customers and groups that trained employees.

This distinction-making was possible because the questions were developed and ordered systematically. They helped organizations requesting presentation room designs to refine their general needs into a series of specific details.

So the questions are designed to be systematic. But only you can be deliberate. That means the checklist isn't something you should rush through, like a menu from a fast-food restaurant. Take your time with the list. Consider what your organization is doing today—and what it may be doing 5 years from now. Consider your objectives and your resources, today and 5 years from now. Remember, if you build a presentation room to solve last year's problems, you may wind up with a room that's obsolete before you can use it.

Presentation Room Questionnaire and Checklist

We present the questionnaire twice. The first time with an explanation of the type of information sought; the second time in a format you can use to start the planning of your own presentation room.

1. Who within your organization will be using the presentation room? This question helps you determine the demands that will be placed on the room. Will salespeople want to use it? Training departments? Advertising and sales promotion groups? Will the president of your organization want to use it to make presentations to security analysts?

Each group that wants to use a presentation room not only increases demand for the room, it may also increase the range of functions the room has to satisfy. You have to know this before design decisions can be made. If, for example, the room is designed solely for training presentations using two-projector productions and a live narrator, it may be of little use to a sales group wanting to stage a "canned" multi-image presentation. Of course, it may be your plan to dedicate the presentation room to a specific function, and that's a perfectly acceptable design decision. But it's a decision that should be made ahead of time, not be default after the fact.

2. What types of audiences will be attending presentations in the room? Customers, prospects, government officials, or other people from outside the company? If so, you may decide that the presentation room has to look like a showcase for your organization. That may mean more money will have to be spent on interior design, furniture and accessories.

If, on the other hand, the room will be used solely for employee instruction presentations, a simple classroom atmosphere may be adequate—and considerably less expensive. If groups both from inside and outside your organization will be using the room, you naturally must find some compromise. Many organizations do this by designing rooms that can be changed from classroom simplicity to conference room prestige by quickly switching furniture and appointments.

3. What size audiences will use the presentation room? The size of your room is determined by the number of people you expect to attend presentations. Since this number will vary according to the group using the room and its purpose, you're going to have to arrive at some average figure. The Kodak engineers found that the best solution to the problem of determining audience size and, thus, room size is to divide audiences (and rooms) into two groups—large and small.

The number of people you can accommodate in a room depends, of course, on how you plan the seating arrangement. If you seat people theatre-style, you can naturally accommodate more than if the seating is at desks or worktables.

The Kodak engineers defined a *large audience* for a presentation room:

- 40 to 45 people seated theatre-style;
- 18 to 24 people seated at desks or worktables.

To accommodate audiences of these sizes, the engineers recommend a room of about 800 square feet, with optimum dimensions of 25 feet by 32 feet. They also recommend that projection distance be kept at between 26 and 28 feet. Projection distances greater than 30 feet should be avoided.

They defined a *small audience* for a presentation room:

- 25 to 30 people seated theatre-style;
- 12 to 18 people seated at desks or worktables.

A room of about 500 square feet, with optimum dimensions of 20 feet by 25 feet, is required to handle the needs of small audiences. A room narrower than 20 feet usually reduces the efficiency of the area.

If your investigations indicate that groups larger than 45 people will regularly attend meetings, you should inquire into the possibility of dividing the audiences into smaller groups. Audiences of 50 or more people usually require facilities beyond those offered by a presentation room.

The illustrations on page 166 and 167 show how a 24-by-22-foot presentation room can be arranged to accommodate a variety of groups with different functions.

4. How often will the presentation room be used? To answer this question, you must gather information on the frequency and duration of presentations. Will the room be used once a week, once a day, three times a day? And will the presentations last an hour, two hours, half a day, all day, all week?

Here again, you're looking not for absolute answers but for typical patterns. You want to come up with figures that account for 80 percent of the presentations to be given. The other 20 percent of the presentations consist of special occasions with unique or unusual requirements.

Your general approach should be to design for the rule and modify for the exceptions. That means you don't include a food service center in your design just because the president holds a luncheon presentation twice a year. When these occasions arise, you simply rearrange the room to accommodate the special requirements.

5. What equipment will be needed? Although this question is fifth on our list, it is the most important one in the questionnaire. It is, in effect, a general question that includes three of the key questions. What sort of visual support will you use in most of your presentations? How will that visual material be presented? How will the narrative be delivered?

The answers to these questions, as we indicated earlier, help you pinpoint the type of equipment you'll want to have. In Chapter 3 we listed the various types of equipment you can choose in putting together a presentation. That discussion applies equally well to choosing equipment for a presentation room. So, once you know what sort of presentations will be given, you have to determine what equipment you're going to need.

Slide projectors. How many? For what type of slides? What type of lenses will you use? For almost all presentations using 2-by-2-inch slides, a projector such as one of the KODAK EKTAGRAPHIC III Slide Projectors is all you need. These projectors can be fitted with either a 7-inch lens or a 9-inch lens, which are adequate for almost all presentation room requirements.

Motion picture projectors. For 16 mm motion picture film, a projector such as the KODAK PAGEANT Projector, fitted with a 200- or 300-watt lamp (depending on the model), and a 2-inch, *f*/1.6 lens is sufficient. This lens can be fitted with an adapter to increase its focal length to 2½ inches.

Lenses. If slides and motion pictures are to be projected side by side, a 7-inch slide projector lens and a 2-inch motion picture lens are recommended because they produce images of almost equal size. For three side-by-side images, a 9-inch lens for the slide projectors and a 2½-inch lens for the 16 mm motion picture projector will work in most situations, but remember to consider the image size you want and the projector distance before you make a decision.

Filmstrip projectors. The majority of filmstrips are made in the standard 35 mm half- or single-frame format; however, various other formats are used with specialized audiovisual equipment for wide-screen effects.

Overhead projectors. With suitable high-contrast line-art cels, overhead projectors can project clean, bright images. Overheads are, therefore, used with large groups and in areas where dimming the lights severely isn't practical or desirable. The principal disadvantages are the need for an operator beside the projector to change cels and the need to place the projector down in front, close to the screen, for most presentations.

6. Where will equipment and supplies be stored? Your presentation room can be much more useful and convenient if all necessary equipment, furniture, spare parts, and maintenance tools are stored within the area itself. In presentation rooms at Kodak, this storage space is usually located alongside the projection room. Large drawers in the presentations room, under the projection booth floor, can provide additional space for items not needed often. See the illustration.

In addition to the factors already discussed, which relate to the particular types of presentation you would be giving, there are other, more general factors to be considered.

7. Acoustics. When designing a presentation room, you face two sound-related problems. The first stems from the need to create an acoustical environment in which a person speaking in a normal tone can be heard by all listeners. The second grows from the desire to keep unwanted sound from entering the room and to keep sounds from the presentation room from disturbing those outside.

To create an acoustically superior presentation room, we suggest that

- the floor be covered with carpet, unless you have a special situation.
- the ceiling be acoustically absorbent.
- the sidewalls be acoustically reflecting, with hard surfaces, such as painted or vinyl fabric-covered plasterboard, demountable metal, or wood paneling. If you want to use display panels, you may want to consider fabric panels or a fabric wall of a material that allows you to change your displays easily.
- the rear wall be acoustically absorbent, constructed of either 2-inch thick fiberglass insulation board covered with an open weave grille cloth, or a wall carpet or carpeting.
- the doors be an airtight frame to eliminate sound transmission.
- the air conditioning be quiet to avoid distracting the audience or interfering with the sound quality.

Large drawers built into a wall provide much needed room for storing wires, spare lamps and parts, and other supplies.

8. Lighting. Lighting requirements can be divided into three categories. Lighting for the lectern area is designed to illuminate the speaker without spilling over into the screen area. This can be accomplished by using two ceiling spotlights. The illumination level is set so that the brightness of the speaker's features is balanced with the image on the screen. The intensity at the lectern top is usually about 15 to 20 footcandles.

Lighting for the seating area should be adjustable. At its high or full setting, the light level should measure between 50 and 80 footcandles. At medium setting, the light level should fall to 5 footcandles. This level allows enough light for working at a desk or for discussion based on information displayed on the screen. At low setting, the level should fall off to 0.4 footcandles. This level is used when major emphasis is on the projected images.

Some presentation rooms also contain lighting that can be used to turn the front of the room into a stage area. These lights are designed to provide 75 to 80 footcandles at a point 30 inches above a finished floor. Track lights or perimeter lights may be desirable if you want to display items on the walls.

9. Electrical power. Considering the equipment and lighting contained within a presentation room, the subject of electrical power requirements and installations is a critical one. Unfortunately, however, it's a topic that falls beyond the scope of this book.

Since every presentation room presents its own set of requirements, it also demands an individual electrical layout. This aspect of planning should be left to your architect, builder, or a specialist in electrical layout from your organization. Your job should be to determine what equipment you're going to install in the room, where you're going to install it, and what the total current draw (amperage) is for each unit. Give this information to your specialist, and let this person take it from there.

10. Furniture. Here again you may be better off leaving the selection of specific items of furniture to specialists. You, however, must make certain that the furniture selected meets two requirements. The first is that it be comfortable. Remember, a folding chair that's moderately comfortable during a 30-minute presentation would become distractingly uncomfortable if it has to be sat in for a 2-hour presentation. So chairs, desks, worktables, and other furniture must be selected with the *last* 15 minutes of your presentations in mind.

The second requirement is that furniture be capable of easy storage if you'll be rearranging pieces for different types of presentations in the room. For the most part, stacking chairs and folding tables are the most suitable.

11. The projection room. In too many presentation rooms, the projection area seems to be an afterthought. Small, crammed with equipment, their shelves and floors a tangle of wires, these rooms are a mockery of efficiency.

A projection room should be a model of efficient work space, a room where there's a place for everything and everything's in its place, including a control panel that can operate every piece of equipment at the push of a button.

Dissolve controls. The number and type of dissolve controls you need for your presentation room depends, of course, on the sophistication of your productions. At the very least, consider a dissolve control with both dissolve and quick-change features. The dissolve rate control and the automatic forward slide change control should also be continuously variable.

Multi-image programmers. Here again, the sophistication of your productions will determine your need for a multi-image programmer. Check with your audio-visual dealer for a description of products and features that meet your needs.

Screens. See page 107 for a discussion of the various types of screens and their uses.

The size of your screen is determined by the distance between screen and audience and the image ratio you plan to use. Once you know these factors, you can choose the projection distance and the lens focal length to suit your situation. For instance, if your back row of viewers is about 40 feet away from the screen, your image height should be *at least* ⅛th of that distance—or 5 feet high in this case. Your next step is to select the lens that gives you that image size on the screen.

If you decide to use two side-by-side 35 mm images, your height stays the same (in our example, 5 feet), and the horizontal measurement for a single image is doubled. This gives you the dimensions for a screen wide enough to accommodate your side-by-side images. For more help in this area, refer to the *KODAK Projection Calculator and Seating Guide For Single- and Multi-Image Presentations* (S-16).

Most presentation rooms use either a built-in screen that can be concealed by a drapery, or a screen that can be lowered from a ceiling-suspended cartridge. Both installations have their advantages and disadvantages, which in the long run tend to balance each other out. So the choice should be made on the basis of which is more practical and convenient in light of your projected requirements. Your choice may also be affected by the need for a chalkboard, flip charts, and similar items.

Tape recorder and playback unit. If you plan to use taped narrations in your presentation, you'll probably want a ¼-inch magnetic tape, stereo playback unit. Depending on the number and nature of your presentations, you may also want to add a high-quality cassette tape recorder and playback unit to your equipment list. The quality of sound from cassette players has improved greatly in the last few years, as has the reliability of built-in synchronization and programmer controls. For simple setups (one or two projectors), consider using a cassette recorder that conforms to ANSI Standard PH 7.4.

Audio mixer. This unit allows you to feed audio signals from several sources into the presentation room's amplifier and speaker system. Most units also allow you to balance the sound input from the various sources. Consider buying a unit with both program and cue channels. The cue channel allows a projectionist to cue up a tape or sound motion picture without disturbing people in the presentation area.

Amplifier. Stick with your local AV dealer's recommendations here. Many recorders have amplifiers built in now. But, whatever your choice, it's a good idea to use those products intended for commercial use.

Loudspeakers. Again, consult with a sound specialist when selecting and placing loudspeakers in your presentation room. There are few things more distracting during a presentation than poor-quality sound. People who must strain to hear what's being said, whether by a live presenter or in a taped narration, soon lose interest in program content. Because sound is so important, having a volume control knob at the lectern can be quite useful.

Keep in mind that spending a lot of money on loudspeakers that have the greatest capacity isn't always the answer. Loudspeakers must be chosen to complement the acoustical qualities of the room in which they'll be used, and only a sound specialist can do that accurately. So don't rush out to buy "watts of power." Get a specialist to help you select loudspeakers that can fill your presentation room with rich, high-fidelity sound and that match with the other components in your system.

Control equipment. One of the greatest advantages of a presentation room is the convenience it offers a presenter. In a well-designed room, he or she has total control over all the elements being used in a presentation. The presenter can start and stop projectors, turn down and bring up room lights, open draperies, lower screens, and in some installations even automatically find a particular slide that's been referred to during a discussion period.

Controls systems make this sort of one-person management possible. Some of these control units are built right into the presentation room podium. (Write to Dept. 412L, Eastman Kodak Company, 343 State Street, Rochester, New York 14650 for the *Remote Control For KODAK Projectors*, S-80-5, for instructions on building a lectern-mounted control system.) Others are wireless units with handheld remote transmitters, which enable a presenter to walk around a presentation area while still retaining control over program elements.

The control systems on the market today are extremely sophisticated—some are capable of controlling up to 40 separate functions. It would be impossible, of course, to describe all the models and features available; it would be somewhat futile too, since new models and features are being introduced daily. If you're interested in purchasing automatic equipment controls, talk to your local audiovisual dealer.

When you do examine specific control units, determine if they control the following functions (providing, of course, that these functions are important to you):

- on/off control of seating area lights and lectern area lights
- lighting level control of seating area lights (either high/medium/low control or variable level control)
- motion picture start/stop
- slide projector controls, including on/off, focus, advance, reverse, and random access (remember, you'll need controls for each projector or for each dissolve pair)
- auxiliary on/off switched outlet
- reel-to-reel tape deck start/stop
- cassette tape deck start/stop

More specifically, an efficient and effective projection room should have

- adequate counter space, especially for the projection equipment. A projection room in which equipment has to be moved every time slide trays have to be changed or film is threaded through a projector is a room that wastes as much time as it saves.

• adequate storage space. Take-up reels, power cords, instruction manuals, blank slides, spare lamps, programs, tool kits–these items plus other essential materials and supplies should be stored in or near the projection room, in easily accessible places. We've been in one projection room where the projectionist had to move three cardboard boxes of supplies in order to set up a stepladder so he could climb up to an almost ceiling-high shelf where he searched through a collection of shoeboxes to find a patch cord needed to link a cassette recorder to an amplifier. Fortunately, there was no rush to set up the equipment. But had this search been launched a few minutes before a presentation was to begin, the results could have been disastrous.

• adequate work room. The best projection rooms have a workbench or work area along the wall behind the projection equipment. This allows a producer to create materials conveniently during the production process. It also allows a projectionist to repair materials during an actual presentation.

• adequate floor space. Often two or more people will have to work in a projection room. Be sure your projection room allows enough space for people to move around without bumping into each other with every step.

• adequate noise control. The noise created by slide tray advances or the operation of a 16 mm motion picture projector should be confined to the projection room.

• adequate projection openings to the main presentation area. Many projection rooms are designed with a single sheet of glass installed along the width of the counter containing the projection equipment. Often, the glass is tilted slightly to reduce undesirable sound and some light reflections. This sort of setup allows projectors to be placed at any convenient and practical location. Other designs provide slots or openings through which images are projected. This type of layout hides the equipment and operators from the view of the audience, an important benefit in some presentations. But a slotted aperture pattern also presents drawbacks. It's more expensive to construct than a single glass window, and it limits your ability to shift equipment to create new projector setups. Also, if the lights are dimmed, the projectionist and equipment in a glass-windowed room are hardly noticeable.

• a means of communication between the seating area and the projection room. Most presentation rooms contain some sort of an intercom system.

• room for change and expansion. Over the years, you'll probably add equipment, so make sure you can move shelves, cut holes, and stack and stock the equipment. Don't tie yourself down to an original design, even though it's a good one.

12. Audience conveniences. The presentation area should be close to certain conveniences participants will need, such as a water fountain and coffee machine, rest rooms, telephones, and coat storage.

Now that we've explained the most important factors to consider in designing a presentation room, we'll repeat the checklist in a more workable format.

Worksheet 3 Projection Room Questionnaire and Checklist

1. Who within your organization will be using the presentation room?
☐ Advertising ☐ Sales ☐ Training ☐ Other
☐ Manufacturing ☐ Executive presentations

2. What types of audiences will be attending presentations in the room?
☐ Employees ☐ Customers ☐ Prospects
☐ Trainees ☐ Media ☐ Other

3. What size audiences will use the presentation room?
Small groups:
☐ 25 to 30 people seated theater style
☐ 12 to 18 people seated at desks or worktables
Large groups:
☐ 40 to 45 people seated theater style
☐ 18 to 24 people seated at desks or worktables
Given the size of the typical audience, the presentation room should have an optimum size of approximately feet by feet.

4. How often will the presentation room be used?
Frequency:
☐ Once a day ☐ Twice a day
☐ Three times a day ☐ More often than three times a day
Weekly frequence:
☐ Once a week ☐ Twice a week
☐ Almost daily ☐ Three times a week
Duration of presentation:
☐ Half hour ☐ Half day ☐ One hour
☐ Full day ☐ Two hours

5. What equipment will be needed?

Slide projectors:	How many?
	For what types of slides?
Motion picture projectors:	How many?
	What film size?
Lenses:	Focal length of slide projector lenses?
	Focal length of motion picture projector lenses?
Filmstrip projector:	Features desired?
Overhead projector:	Features desired?
Dissolve controls:	How many?
	Features desired?
Multi-image programmer:	To control how many projectors?
	Features desired?
Screens:	Surface type?
	Image ratio?
	Projection distance?
	Focal length of lenses?
	Final image area size?
	Screen size?
Tape recorder and playback units:	¼-inch, reel to reel?
	Features desired?
	Cassette unit?
	Features desired?
Audio mixer:	Features desired?
Amplifier:	Features desired?
Loudspeakers:	Number needed?
	Power output?
	Special requirements?

Controls:
Lighting: ☐ lectern area ☐ seating area ☐ stage area
☐ Lighting level ☐ Motion picture start/stop
☐ Slide projector on/off ☐ focus ☐ advance ☐ reverse
☐ random access ☐ Auxiliary on/off switched outlet
☐ Reel-to-reel tape deck start/stop
☐ Cassette tape deck start/stop ☐ Permanent installation
☐ portable transmitter

6. Where will equipment and supplies be stored?

7. Acoustics: Indicate covering and/or construction for:	Floor
	Ceiling
	Sidewalls
	Rear wall
	Doors
8. Lighting: Indicate requirements for:	Lectern area
	Seating area
	Stage area
9. Electrical power:	Determine requirements and layout in conjunction with electrical specialist.

10. Furniture:

Chairs:	How Many?	Style?
Tables:	How Many?	Style?
Other:		

11. Projection room:
☐ Counter space
☐ Storage space
☐ Work area
☐ Noise Control

Have you allowed for adequate:
☐ Floor space
☐ Communication from projection room to seating area

12. Audience conveniences:
Are the following conveniences close by?
☐ Rest rooms ☐ Water fountain, coffee machine, etc.
☐ Telephones ☐ Provisions to bring in refreshments
☐ Coat storage

Room, Please

If you plan on building a presentation room, you also should plan on establishing procedures for reserving and using the room.

If you don't, you'll soon find that this special audiovisual center has become just another conversation pit–part lounge, part lunch room, part general work room and part temporary storage area.

You'll also find that some of the people who casually use the room won't respect its original purpose. They'll leave slide projectors and other equipment out on tables. Or they'll leave chalkboards covered with the notes, numbers and diagrams of a brainstorming session. Their styrofoam coffee cups and littered ashtrays will be scattered throughout the room. And if they need more space, they'll push tables, chairs and lecturn "out of the way," which usually means jammed into a corner or along a wall.

Malicious behavior? No. It just seems to be human nature to prefer working in a large room rather than a small office. It also seems to be organizational nature to leave the cleanup to someone else.

Unfortunately, once this work room atmosphere takes hold, a presentation room begins to lose its effectiveness. Rather than being an area set aside exclusively for communication, it becomes a place people go when they want to be away from desks and phones.

You can prevent this sort of misuse, though, by establishing simple procedures for reserving and using the presentation room.

Central to these procedures is the Conference Room Reservation, a form the person requesting the room must fill out *in advance* of a presentation date. This form asks for information on when the room is needed, the length of time it will be in use, the number of people who will be attending the presentation, the type of equipment needed, and the seating pattern required. (A sample form, based on one used by a number of groups within Eastman Kodak Company, is reproduced.)

Just as important as the reservation form is a person who can serve as a presentation room coordinator. This person will book–and confirm–all reservations (usually on a first-come, first-served basis) and arrange for seating and equipment requirements. In some organizations, this person also serves as a clearing center for messages to or from presentation participants or attendees.

This coordinator isn't expected to stand guard over the room, however. If you'll have regulations governing the use of the room–such as those covering maximum length of time a room can be reserved or procedures to be followed for ordering refreshments–these should be printed *in a prominent spot* on the reservation form.

All this may sound like a lot of bureaucratic make-work, an attempt to inflate someone's position through paperwork. But it's not. When you consider the time, money and effort that go into planning and constructing a presentation room, you'll realize it's worth a little extra effort to make your original intentions stick.

Confirmation

Conference Room Reservation

Management & General Education–Corporate Relations Division
Facilities at Kodak Office, 6th Floor, Bldg. 16

To: Date / /

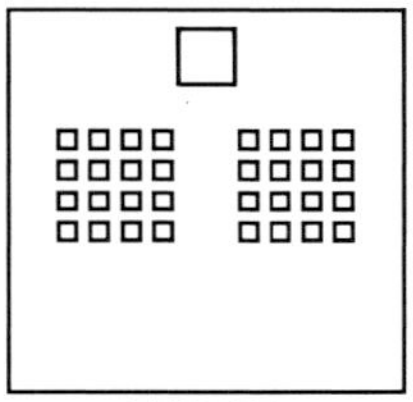

THEATRE

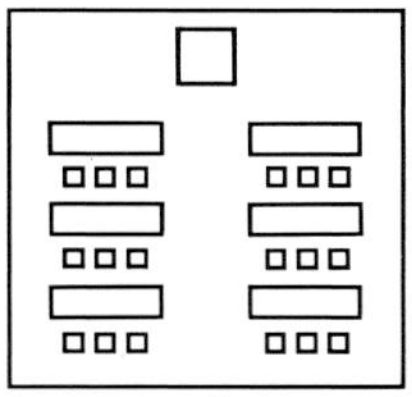

CLASSROOM (WithTables)

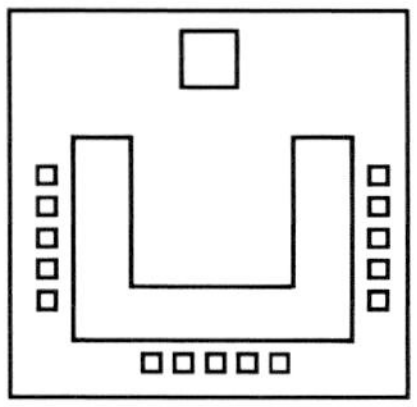

CONFERENCE

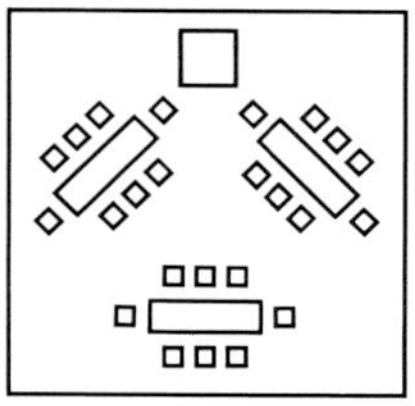

MODULAR

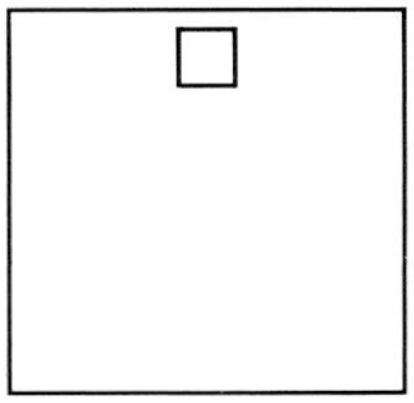

OTHER

At your request, M&GE Conference__________, 6th Floor, Bldg. 16, Kodak Office, has been reserved for your use on the following schedule:

____

You stated your equipment requirements to be:______________________________

____

The room will be set up to accommodate__________people in the fashion indicated at the left.

Conference room space is valuable. If plans change and this room is no longer needed, please call Jane Smith (Ext. 55555).

Experience has led us to establish these room use "rules of thumb."

1. We will reserve rooms only within four weeks of desired use.

2. We will not commit a conference room to one group for more than one solid week at a time.

3. We cannot honor requests for regular commitments beyond one month, e.g., weekly, monthly, meetings, etc.

4. Special refreshment needs must be arranged by you through the cafeteria. M&GE personnel cannot serve as host or hostess.

5. Meetings will be interrupted only for calls considered urgent. Conference room users are urged to provide the M&GE Receptionist with a roster of meeting participants to facilitate this. A telephone message board is provided.

6. Audiovisual or other equipment needs can often be filled with sufficient advanced information. A requesting department representative should contact Jane Smith (Ext. 55555) well in advance of the meeting to check out such services and learn what can and cannot be done by M&GE–the responsibility for assuring that audiovisual equipment is ready for use when it is needed remains yours. We will try to be of service, but we will not assume this responsibility. A special projectionist is not available.

Presentation Room Plan 22′x24′

Projection Room
Allow for ample counter-space. Also allow room to store supplies and other materials you may need either just before or during a presentation.

Storage Room
You'll need room to store large items such as extra tables and chairs, display materials, flipcharts and other items not used in the presentation room on a regular basis.

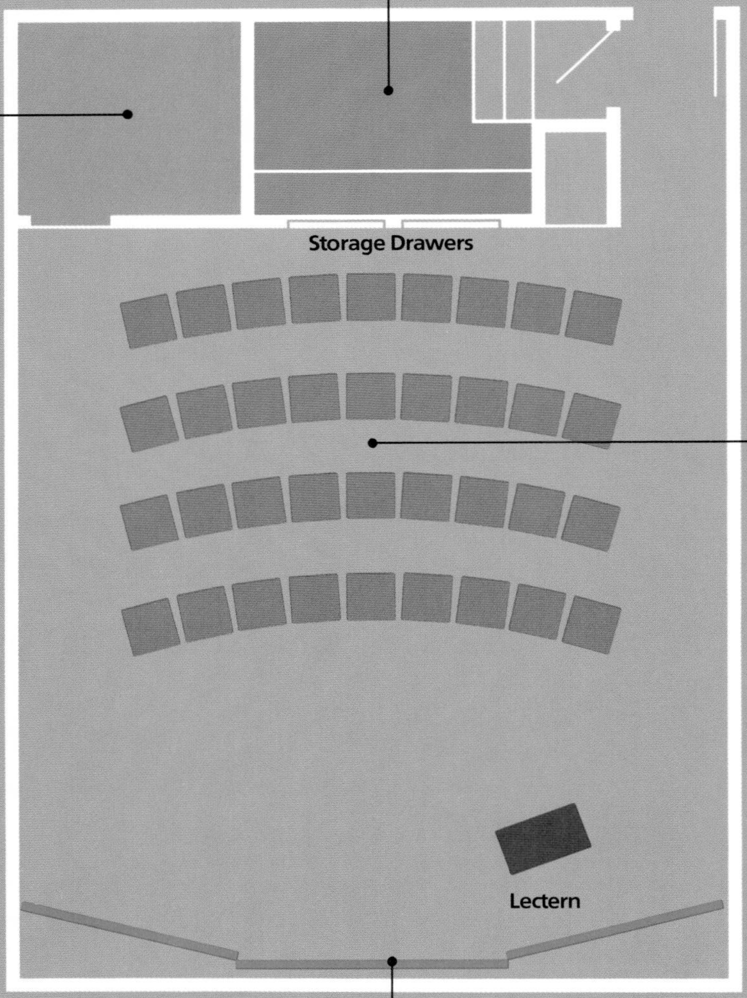

Theatre Seating Plan

Presentation Room
The size of the presentation area should be based on the size of expected audiences. Allow for a presentation area of at least 20 by 24 feet for audiences up to 30 people.

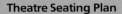

Screen
Selecting the right size and type of screen shouldn't be left to chance. Study the recommendations on page 175.

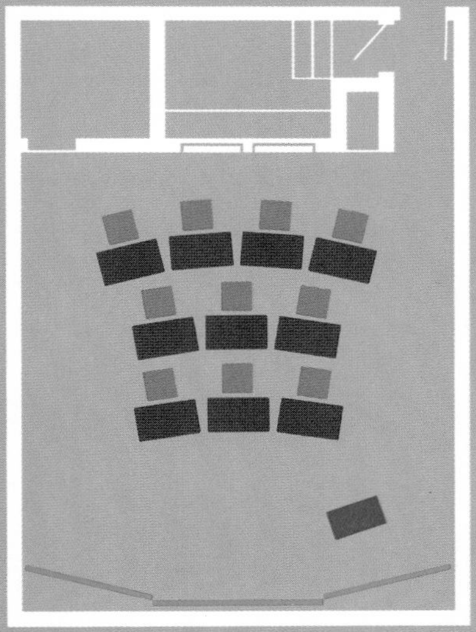
Row-Table Seating Plan

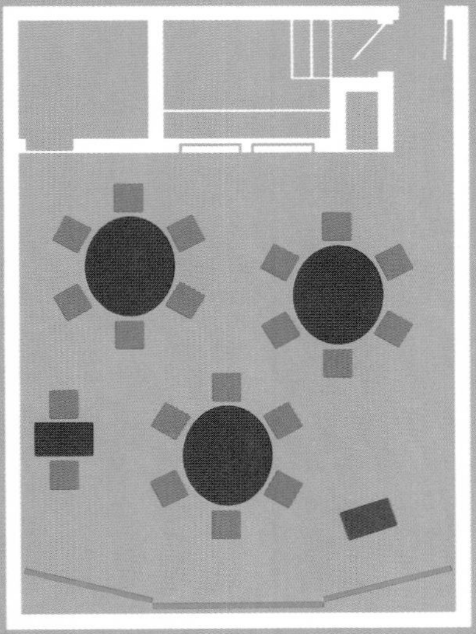
Work Group Seating Plan

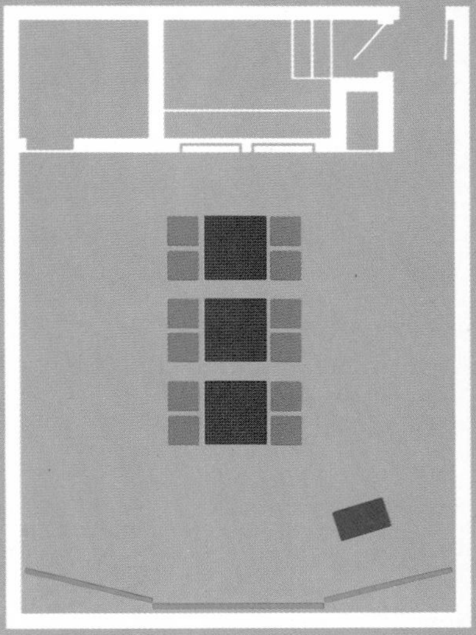
Conference Table Seating Plan

For GTE, Happiness Is a Detailed Plan

GTE's main presentation room allows for multi-image, motion picture and video projection.

The more time you spend planning a presentation room, the happier you'll be with it when it's finished.

Just ask the people at the GTE Products Corporation facility in Batavia, New York. They spent four months planning every aspect of their four-room presentation complex–from the wiring layouts to the size of the tables they'd use–and now that it's finished, they're more than satisfied with the results.

"If we had to do it over again," says Bernie Laplante, manager of technical services at the facility and one of the people who helped in the planning, "we wouldn't change much."

To fully appreciate Laplante's statement, you have to know that when he and his colleagues started their planning, all they wanted was a site to hold an annual sales convention. Unhappy with the results they had had using hotel conference areas, they decided to take an unused section of their manufacturing plant and turn it into a convention hall. It seemed like a good idea, so good in fact that they quickly realized the convention was only a current need. They began to see the potential for enlarging their site into a year-round, all-purpose presentation area.

"Very early on," says Harlan Lippincott, manager of the group's technical training department, "we began to determine what needs we would have beyond the sales convention." What they found were requirements ranging from technical training to press conferences to meetings of community groups. "It became obvious," adds Lippincott, "that just about every group in our plant, at one time or another, might have a need for a presentation area. At that point, even though we kept our planning focused on the specific needs for our sales convention, we also decided to make our work the foundation for an overall presentation area."

To achieve this objective, the GTE planners strove for flexibility. Their key decision in pursuit of this goal was to move beyond planning for a single room and, instead, construct a complex consisting of four rooms. One was designed for general presentations, a second room was designed for technical training. These rooms are served by a common workroom and storage area situated between them. A fourth room, for product demonstrations and displays, is also part of the complex, but is not a presentation room *per se*.

The general presentation room is the more flexible of the two main rooms. It measures 36 feet by 30 feet, with a 10-foot high ceiling. This area is large enough to hold 105 people seated theatre-style or between 35 and 40 people if the room is arranged to accommodate work groups. In the front of the room, GTE uses a white projection wall for image displays. To the left of this screen area stands a podium; to the right of it, a pedestal holding a color television set (GTE manufactures and sells Sylvania television products and uses video extensively in its presentations). The projection booth at the rear of the room contains counter space sufficient to hold 25 to 30 slide projectors plus a motion picture projector. It's also equipped with a multi-image programmer, advanced dissolve controls, a tape recorder/playback unit, an audio mixer, and controls for the presentation room lighting.

"This is the equipment we needed to put on our sales convention," adds Laplante, "but it's not all the equipment we'll eventually need. Our plan is to purchase additional equipment over a 2-year period, but only as specific needs arise.

This approach makes it a lot easier to control budgets and expenditures. It also keeps you from buying equipment in a rush of enthusiasm, only to find out later that you really didn't need it."

The sound level of the room is controlled by using acoustical tile on the ceiling, carpeting on the floor, and insulated walls covered by textured panels. (The textured panels are made of a special weave that provides a strong adherence surface for quick-stick fasteners. Presenters routinely affix posters, signs, and other visual displays to the walls. Even heavier objects, such as a small writing surface next to the telephone, are affixed to the wall using only quick-stick fasteners.)

Provisions have been made for the easy posting of displays and messages.

The emphasis in the projection room is on ample counterspace.

To further reduce the possibility of interruptions from unwanted sound, telephones in the presentation area and the projection booth are equipped with flashing lights instead of bells. Additionally, GTE used flexible ducts in its air-conditioning installation to cut down vibration noises.

The sound that is wanted in the room—be it a speaker's voice or the narration from a slide, film, or videotape program—is carried through four air-suspended loudspeakers.

Lighting is provided by a combination of fluorescent and incandescent lights. Fluorescent lights are used when full lighting is desired; dimmable incandescent drop lights are used during presentations. A series of dimmable track lights, both spots and floods, are used along the front of the room to illuminate the speaker and a small stage area.

Wiring cutouts.

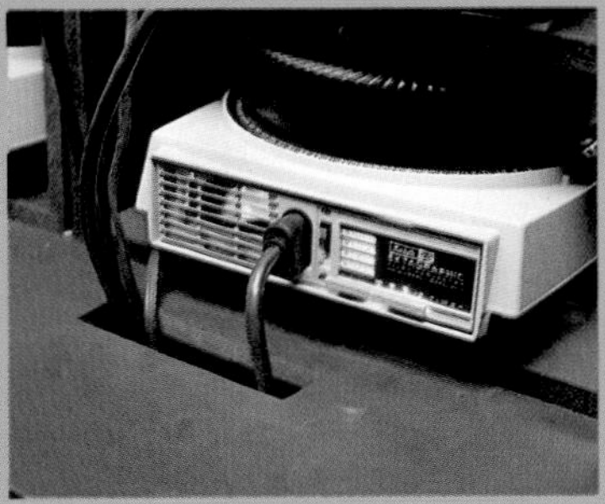

Glass separating projection booth from presentation room is slanted to reduce glare and noise.

Behind the scenes, in the projection booth, the work area measures 22 feet by 6 feet. "We determined this size by visiting presentation rooms in other companies and copying what seemed most practical and workable," says Lippincott. Some of the other projection booth construction ideas picked up by the GTE planners include:

- the use of rectangular cutouts in the countertop that holds presentation projectors (to make it easier to route equipment wires);
- the need to slant the glass that serves as the projection opening to the room to cut down noise and light reflection in the presentation room;
- the need to paint the rear wall of the projection booth a dark color to cut down on light reflection from within the booth.

With its large seating capacity and extensive projection booth capabilities, the general presentation room is used for GTE sales conventions, management meetings, conferences, and sales training programs. The special features included in the room also make it ideal for special activities. For example, because the room is ringed with phone jacks, it's used for periodic "sales blitzes," in which salespeople call key customers throughout the country in what amounts to a 1-day sales marathon. Sales totals are entered into a video character generator set up in the projection booth, then relayed to a television monitor in the front of the room, giving participants an up-to-the-minute report on the success of their efforts.

These activities keep the room in use at least 3 days a week, and scheduling has not yet become a serious problem. Laplante, however, projects a rapid increase in the number of presentations that will be given in the room, especially in the area of sales training.

"Within the next year," he says, "we're going to have to institute some sort of system to handle scheduling. It's all part of our growth plan."

Laplante and his colleagues are expansive when they talk about the potential uses of the general presentation room. They talk about what they could do and what they might do as they envision the groups and activities that may soon be using the room.

But their tone of voice and choice of words change just a bit when they talk about the technical training presentation room. It's not because the room doesn't have the potential of the general presentation room, it's just that the potential of the training area is being realized much more quickly.

"We know what we can do in here," says Laplante. The room is currently being used to train the division's field engineers and its sales and service support people, as well as service managers from GTE's distributor network. The GTE training people are also looking at programs for service people from retail dealers. "It's just a matter of developing the programs for the groups that we'd like to train."

Training room contains both a seating area and room for workbenches.

One of the reasons the technical training presentation room has been so immediately successful is its layout. Although totally open, the 32-by-30-foot room is divided into discrete areas. The center portion of the room is arranged in classroom style, with rows of tables and chairs facing a large white projection wall. This area is used for lectures and for audio-visual presentations.

On either side of the classroom seating are hands-on work areas. These areas are furnished with movable workbenches, equipped with all the diagnostic and repair tools trainees will need to complete their instruction. Each workbench also contains a small television monitor, through which conventional and programmed instruction programs are presented.

There are 12 benches in all, six on each side of the room. "When we schedule a program," says Laplante, "we usually have no more than three people at a workbench. That gives us a maximum training group of 36 people." When only the classroom seating is used, the room can accommodate 40 people.

Trainees can watch techniques being demonstrated on screen, then repeat them at workbench.

In almost all cases, the technical training presentations are accompanied by visuals, either slides or videotape programs produced by the GTE trainers. The slide presentations are usually three-projector productions, although some presentations may require up to six projectors. The video presentations are beamed onto the projection wall through a ceiling-suspended video projection system.

Video cameras also can be used in the training room when a trainer wants to show actual materials–for example, miniature electronic components–without having the trainees leave their seats. The video signal is transmitted through jacks located at baseboard level throughout the room. It goes through a signal modulator and distributor located in the work area, where it's relayed back to the video projection equipment or to the television monitors located at the workbenches.

Other visual information, such as electrical schematics, diagnostic flowcharts, service literature, and even the sketches and notes of an instructor, are displayed on a series of movable display boards designed by the GTE planners. The four 6-by-8-foot boards, mounted one behind the other, ride in metal tracks that stretch across the front of the room. Three of the display boards are covered with fabric to allow the mounting of materials using quick-stick fasteners. The outermost board is a specially coated hardboard surface that trainers can write on using water-soluble felt-tipped markers.

When the information contained on one of the boards is needed, the trainer merely pulls it to a spot where it will dominate the attention of the trainees. (Because the display boards are mounted one in front of the other, a trainer can affix materials on the textured boards and then leave them, semi-concealed, behind the outer "chalkboard.") When the material has been covered, the instructor pushes the display board back into its original position.

"The arrangement is actually very simple, but it's also extremely effective," says Laplante. "It enables us to use a wide variety of printed materials and enlarged schematic drawings. And it makes using them easier for the trainer. He can mount them on the display boards before a training session begins, leave them there without having them distract the trainees, then use them when he needs them. And when he's finished, he just pushes them back out of the way."

Training materials are mounted on semi-concealed display boards.

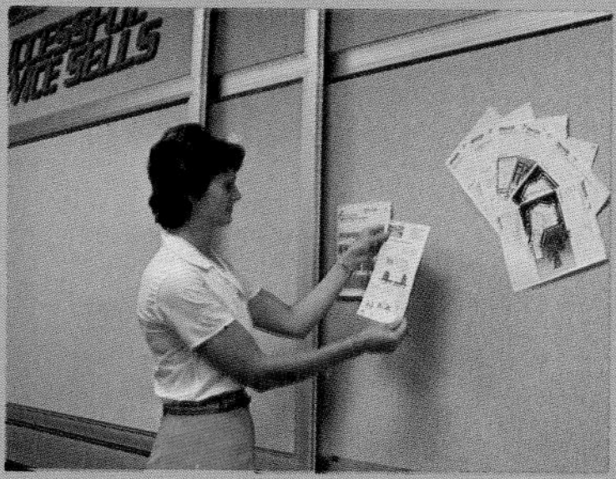

To fit all this furniture and equipment into the room, the GTE planners used a model of the room, scaled 1 inch to the foot, which they furnished with wood blocks scaled to the size of the desks and workbenches. They called this miniature version of their training room the "doll house." Working with their "doll house," they pushed the blocks around, into one configuration and then another, until finally they came up with a layout that gave them the greatest flexibility and the most pleasing layout.

Lippincott says it cost them about $200 to $300 to build and furnish their "doll house," but he adds the money was well spent. They still use the model when they have to rearrange the room for special groups or presentations. "It saves a lot of time," he says, "and it's a lot easier to move around the blocks rather than the actual furniture. I recommend this practice to anyone who's trying to devise a layout for a presentation room."

Soundproofed doors lead into each presentation room from the common work and storage area situated between them. A third door allows access to the room without the need to walk through the presentation rooms.

The work/storage area holds no surprises. It's equipped with desks, workbenches, files, and storage shelves, the objects you'd expect to see in such an area. Stackable chairs, folding tables, and extra equipment are stored wherever space is available. In fact, the only unusual piece of equipment in the room is a video signal modulator and distributor designed and built by GTE engineers. The unit links the almost four miles of closed-circuit cable running behind the walls of the four-room complex.

Like many other aspects of the presentation area, the signal distributor is a unit whose potential GTE has only begun to explore. "Someday," says Wayne French, the GTE engineer who designed the unit and supervised its building and installation, "we may be transmitting presentations to offices throughout the building or to GTE sites throughout the country. Or we may be receiving presentations originating elsewhere. Whatever may come, we're ready."

At first, the GTE planners considered building separate work areas for each presentation room, but then decided against it. "We found it would be much more efficient and economical to have a common work area," says Laplante. "That allows us to share equipment and supplies. It also allows work to go on, even during presentations."

If the GTE presentation complex sounds like a dream come true, well, you're almost right. It's more accurate to say it's a plan come to life–a comprehensive plan that's resulted in an efficient, flexible, totally useable presentation site.

Four miles of closed-circuit cable link the four-room complex.

Further Reading

Numerous books on public speaking are available from your local book stores or library. Not surprisingly, most cover the same general topics, from how to develop your ideas to how to handle stage fright. However, certain books give more emphasis to particular topics, while others may cover these topics briefly only to give more emphasis in other areas.

So if you're interested in reading books on public speaking, you'd be wise to check not only tables of contents, but also individual chapters. Browse. Pick out books that cover those subjects that interest you–or will benefit you–the most.

How many books will you have to read? One may be enough. Two or three at most. Remember, your goal isn't to become an expert on public speaking. Your goal is to become a proficient speaker. Reading can't accomplish that, only practice can. So once you know the basics, put down the books and start making presentations.

The books listed below are representative of those dealing with public speaking. Others not mentioned in this list may serve your needs equally well.

Hegarty, Edward. *The Successful Speaker's Planning Guide.* New York: McGraw-Hill Book Company, 1970.

Quick, John. *A Short Book on the Subject of Speaking*. New York: McGraw-Hill Book Company, 1978.

Snell, Frank. *How To Stand Up and Speak Well in Business.* New York: Cornerstone Library, 1974.

Stone, Janet, and Bachner, Jane. *Speaking Up.* New York: McGraw-Hill Book Company, 1977.

Tack, Alfred. *How To Speak Well in Public.* Grand Rapids: Baker Book House, 1955, 1973.

Projection Distance Table for KODAK EKTAGRAPHIC Slide Projectors

(Projection distances are approximate and are measured from projector gate to screen.)

Nominal Aperture Dimensions* of 2 x 2-Inch Slide Mounts

Nominal Lens Focal Length (in inches)

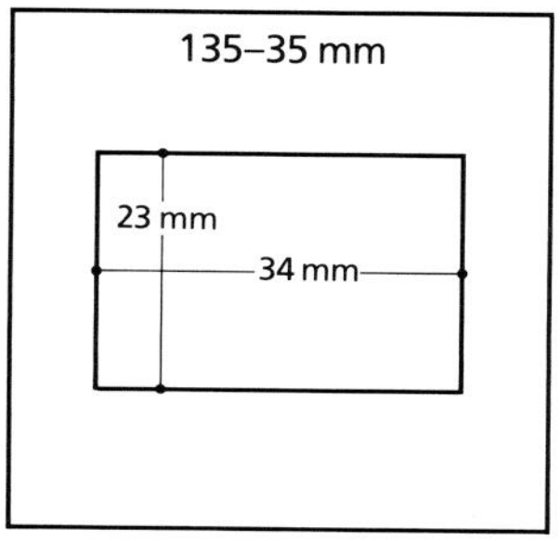

Approximate Projection Distances (in feet)

Screen Image Height (in inches)	1.4	2	3	4	5	7	9	11	4 to 6 (Zoom)
40	5½	8	11½	15½	19½	27	35	42½	15½ to 23½
48	6½	9	14	18½	23	32½	41½	51	18½ to 27½
56	7½	10½	16	21½	27	37½	48½	59	21½ to 32
80	10½	15	23	30½	38	53	69	84	30½ to 45½
96	12½	18	27	36½	45½	64	82	100	36½ to 55

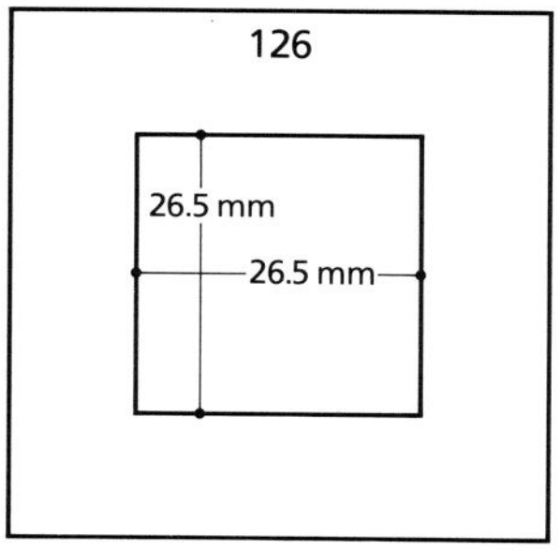

Approximate Projection Distances (in feet)

Screen Image Height (in inches)	1.4	2	3	4	5	7	9	11	4 to 6 (Zoom)
40	4½	6½	10	13½	17	23½	30½	37	13½ to 20
50	6	8½	12½	16½	21	29	37½	46	16½ to 25
60	7	10	15	20	25	34½	44½	55	20 to 30
72	8½	12	18	23½	29½	41½	54	65	23½ to 35½
84	9½	14	20½	27½	34½	48	62	75½	27½ to 41½

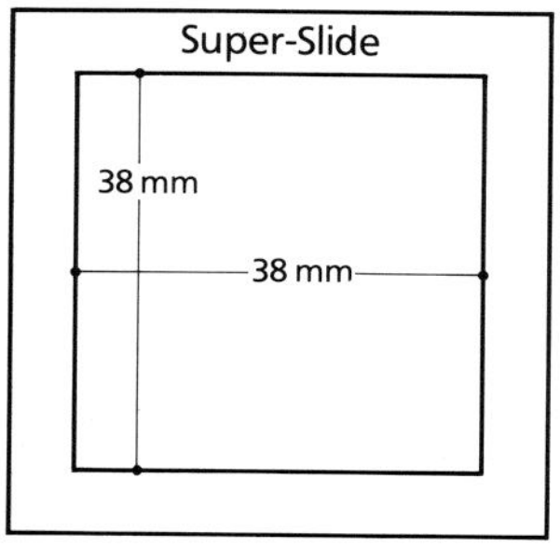

Approximate Projection Distances (in feet)

Screen Image Height (in inches)	1.4	2	3	4	5	7	9	11	4 to 6 (Zoom)
40	3½	5	7	9½	12	16½	21½	26½	9½ to 14½
50	4	6	9	12	14½	20½	26½	32½	12 to 17½
60	5	7	10½	14	17½	24½	31½	38½	14 to 21
72	6	8½	12½	16½	21	29	37½	46	16½ to 25
84	7	9½	14½	19½	24	34	43½	53	19½ to 29

Note: Kodak supplies a 2½-inch EKTANAR Projection Lens (not shown). It is designed especially for use in study carrels and in small rear-projection cabinets. With a standard 35 mm slide, the lens produces an 8-inch-wide image in a 26-inch distance (back of projector to the front of the screen). Image sizes over 12 inches wide are not recommended.

*Dimension tolerances may vary with mounts of different sizes and manufacture.